my **revision** notes

WJEC EDUQAS GCSE (9–1)

ENGLISH LANGUAGE

Jane Sheldon

HODDER
EDUCATION
AN HACHETTE UK COMPANY

The publisher would like to thank the following for permission to reproduce copyright material:

Acknowledgements:
p.10: Graham Greene: from *Brighton Rock* (Vintage Classics, 1938), originally published by Vintage Classics, used with permission from David Higham Associates; **p.11, p.67: Charles Dickens:** letter from *The Daily News* (4 February 1846); **p.12: Larisa Brown:** from '100 toddlers expelled by nurseries for being violent: Children as young as one sent home for attacking toddlers and teachers', http://www. dailymail.co.uk/news/article-3516600/100-toddlers-expelled-nurseries-violent-Children-young-one-sent-home-attacking-toddlers-teachers.html (*Daily Mail*, 31 March 2016), © MailOnline; **pp.13–14, p.20, p.31, p.36: Ian McEwan:** from *Enduring Love* (Jonathan Cape, 1997), reprinted by permission of The Random House Group Limited © 1997; **p. 14, 48: Pat Barker:** from *The Man Who Wasn't There* (1989, Penguin), used with permission; **pp.15–16, p.24: Mary Lawson:** from *The Other Side of the Bridge* (Chatto & Windus, 2007), reprinted by permission of The Random House Group Limited © 2006; **p.18: Roald Dahl:** from 'The Hitchhiker' (Penguin Books Ltd, 1977), originally published by Penguin in *The Collected Short Stories of Roald Dahl*. Used with permission from David Higham Associates; **pp.21–22, p.23: F. Scott Fitzgerald:** from *The Great Gatsby* (Penguin Book Ltd., 1925), public domain; **p.25: Truman Capote:** from *In Cold Blood*, reprinted by permission of Literary Executor Truman Capote Estate; **p.26: Roddy Doyle:** from *Paddy Clarke Ha Ha Ha* (Vintage, 1993), used with permission from John Sutton Management; **p.27: Sylvia Plath:** from *The Bell Jar* (Faber & Faber, 1963), extract published with fair use; **p.37: Franz Kafka:** from: *The Trial* (1925), www.online-literature.com/ franz-kafka/the-trial/1/, printed with permission; **p.38–39: Ian McEwan:** from *Amsterdam* (Jonathan Cape, 1998), reproduced by permission of The Random House Group Ltd. ©1998; **p.40: Reginald Hill:** from *On Beulah Height* (1998, HarperCollins), used with permission from United Agents; **p.42: Nick Hornby**: from *High Fidelity* (Penguin Books Ltd, 2000), copyright © Nick Hornby, 1998; **p.55: Ian Cobain:** from 'Tough case to crack: the mystery of Britain's falling crime rate', https://www.theguardian.com/uk-news/2014/aug/31/tough-case-mystery-britains-falling-crime-rate (*Guardian*, 31 August 2014), copyright Guardian News & Media Ltd 2017; **p.62:** 'About us' from 'Vale Karate' website, www.valekarate.com/about-us; **p.64**: Charles Dickens: from *Sketches by Boz* (1836), public domain; **p.64, p.65:** Fanny Burney: 'Account from Paris of a Terrible Operation, 1812', Letter to Esther Burney (March 22–June 1812), public domain; **p.67, p.73: Lydia Maria Francis Child and Eliza Leslie:** from *The Little Girl's Own Book* (1847), public domain; **p.67, p.70:** 'The Coronation of Queen Victoria' from *Hereford Times* (30 June 1838), British Newspaper Archive; **p.70: Danny Boyle:** from 'Kate Middleton's new royal baby Princess Charlotte meets Queen – as it happened', http://www.telegraph.co.uk/news/uknews/princess-charlotte/11585153/Kate-Middletons-new-royal-baby-Princess-Charlotte-meets-Queen-as-it-happened.html (*Telegraph*, 5 May 2015), © Telegraph Media Group Limited 2015; **p.71:** Emily Thornwell: from *The Lady's Guide to Perfect Gentility, in Manners, Dress and Conversation* (Derby & Jackson, 1857), public domain; **p.73:** 'Why does gender-stereotyped toy marketing matter?' from 'Let Toys be Toys' website, http://lettoysbetoys.org.uk/why-it-matters/, used with permission; **p.75: Virginia Tatnall Peacock:** from 'Famous American Belles of the Nineteenth Century' (1901); **p.76:** '6 ways to tell you're with the person you should marry, according to science' from 'Mic' website, https://mic.com/articles/110744/6-ways-to-tell-you-re-with-the-person-you-should-marry-according-to science#.uQA2D5fwV, used with permission.

Photo credits:

p.47 © Anyka - Fotolia; **p.62** © Ingram Publishing Limited; **p.77** © Imagestate Media (John Foxx).

Although every effort has been made to ensure that website addresses are correct at time of going to press, Hodder Education cannot be held responsible for the content of any website mentioned. It is sometimes possible to find a relocated web page by typing in the address of the home page for a website in the URL window of your browser.

Orders: please contact Bookpoint Ltd, 130 Milton Park, Abingdon, Oxon OX14 4SB.
Telephone: (44) 01235 827720.
Fax: (44) 01235 400401.
Lines are open 9.00–17.00, Monday to Saturday, with a 24-hour message answering service.
Visit our website at www.hoddereducation.co.uk

© Jane Sheldon 2017

First published in 2017 by
Hodder Education
An Hachette UK Company,
Carmelite House, 50 Victoria Embankment
London EC4Y 0DZ

Impression number	5	4	3	2	1
Year	2021	2020	2019	2018	2017

Cover photo © Jacquie Boyd from Debut Art Agency

Illustrations by Integra Software Services Pvt. Ltd., Pondicherry, India

Typeset in Bembo Std Regular 11/13 by Integra Software Services Pvt. Ltd., Pondicherry, India

Printed in Spain

ISBN 9781510417762

Get the most from this book

Everyone has to decide his or her own revision strategy, but it is essential to review your work, learn it and test your understanding. These Revision Notes will help you to do that in a planned way, topic by topic. Use this book as the cornerstone of your revision and don't hesitate to write in it – personalise your notes and check your progress by ticking off each section as you revise.

Tick to track your progress

Use the revision planner on pages 4 and 5 to plan your revision, topic by topic. Tick each box when you have:

- revised and understood a topic
- tested yourself
- practised the exam questions and checked your answers

You can also keep track of your revision by ticking off each topic heading in the book. You may find it helpful to add your own notes as you work through each topic.

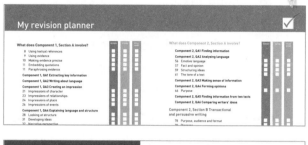

Features to help you succeed

Exam tips

Expert tips are given throughout the book to help you polish your exam technique in order to maximise your chances in the exam.

Typical mistakes

The author identifies the typical mistakes candidates make and explains how you can avoid them.

Test yourself

These short, knowledge-based questions provide the first step in testing your learning. Answers are at the back of the book.

Definitions and key words

Clear, concise definitions of essential key terms are provided where they first appear.

Key words from the specification are highlighted in bold throughout the book.

How to prepare for the exam

Exam advice is provided for each topic. Use it to consolidate your revision and practise your exam skills.

Assessment comment

Throughout, there are comments and annotations which explain exactly why grades are awarded and what is good about the responses that are provided.

My revision planner

REVISED   TESTED   EXAM READY

What does Component 2, Section A involve?

REVISED   TESTED   EXAM READY

The exam papers

You will have to complete two examination papers.

Component 1: 1 hour and 45 minutes
(80 marks – 40 per cent of your GCSE)

Twentieth-century Literature Reading and Creative Prose Writing

Section A
- You will need to answer questions about an extract (of about 60–100 lines) of literature from the twentieth century.
- You will have one hour for this section: 10 minutes to read and 50 minutes to answer.
- It is worth 40 marks.

Section B
- You will complete a creative writing task from a selection of four titles.
- You will have 45 minutes for this section: 10 minutes to plan and 35 minutes to write.
- It is worth 40 marks.

Component 2: 2 hours (80 marks – 60 per cent of your GCSE)

Nineteenth and Twenty-first-century Non-fiction Reading and Transactional/ Persuasive Writing

Section A
- You will need to answer questions about two extracts, totalling about 900–1,200 words, of high-quality non-fiction writing from the nineteenth and twenty-first centuries.
- You have one hour for this section: 10 minutes to read and 50 minutes to answer.
- It is worth 40 marks.

Section B
- You will need to complete two transactional/ persuasive writing tasks.
- You have one hour for this section, divided into 30 minutes for each question: 5 minutes planning and 25 minutes writing on each task.
- Each task is worth 20 marks.

All of the following skills will be tested:

Across Section A, you will be tested on your ability to:
- identify and interpret information and ideas
- analyse how writers use language and structure to achieve effects
- evaluate the content of a text
- support what you say with evidence from the text.

In the Component 2 exam, you will have two texts, so you will also have to synthesise information from both and compare writers' ideas.

In Section B, you will be tested on your ability to:
- communicate clearly, effectively and imaginatively
- write appropriately for purpose and audience
- organise your writing effectively
- use a range of vocabulary and sentence structures
- spell and punctuate accurately.

You should have noticed that, although both examinations are worth 80 marks, there is a slightly heavier weighting on the non-fiction reading and writing in Component 2 (60 per cent) than on the literature and creative writing in Component 1 (40 per cent).

Countdown to my exams

6–8 weeks to go

- Start by looking at the specification — make sure you know exactly what material you need to revise and the style of the examination. Use the revision planner on pages 4 and 5 to familiarise yourself with the topics.
- Organise your notes, making sure you have covered everything on the specification. The revision planner will help you to group your notes into topics.
- Work out a realistic revision plan that will allow you time for relaxation. Set aside days and times for all the subjects that you need to study, and stick to your timetable.
- Set yourself sensible targets. Break your revision down into focused sessions of around 40 minutes, divided by breaks. These Revision Notes organise the basic facts into short, memorable sections to make revising easier.

REVISED ☐

2–6 weeks to go

- Read through the relevant sections of this book and refer to the exam tips, how to prepare for the exam, typical mistakes and key terms. Tick off the topics as you feel confident about them. Highlight those topics you find difficult and look at them again in detail.
- Test your understanding of each topic by working through the 'Test yourself' questions in the book. Look up the answers at the back of the book.
- Make a note of any problem areas as you revise, and ask your teacher to go over these in class.
- Look at past papers. They are one of the best ways to revise and practise your exam skills. Write or prepare planned answers to the exam practice questions provided in this book.
- Track your progress using the revision planner and give yourself a reward when you have achieved your target.

REVISED ☐

One week to go

- Try to fit in at least one more timed practice of an entire past paper and seek feedback from your teacher, comparing your work closely with the mark scheme.
- Check the revision planner to make sure you haven't missed out any topics. Brush up on any areas of difficulty by talking them over with a friend or getting help from your teacher.
- Attend any revision classes put on by your teacher. Remember, he or she is an expert at preparing people for exams.

REVISED ☐

The day before the exam

- Flick through these Revision Notes for useful reminders, for example the exam tips, how to prepare for the exam, typical mistakes and key terms.
- Check the time and place of your exam.
- Make sure you have everything you need — extra pens and pencils, tissues, a watch, bottled water, sweets.
- Allow some time to relax and have an early night to ensure you are fresh and alert for the exam.

REVISED ☐

My exams

GCSE English Language Component 1

Date:...

Time:...

Location:...

GCSE English Language Component 2

Date:...

Time:...

Location:...

What does Component 1, Section A involve?

What you have to do

Component 1, Section A has five questions about an extract from a novel written in the twentieth century. There are 40 marks available.

You have about an hour to complete this section. It is important that you finish in 60 minutes, because you need the remaining 45 minutes to write your response to Section B.

As a guide, you should spend around 10 minutes reading the text carefully, then about 50 minutes answering the questions on it. Obviously, the quicker you can read, the more time you have to answer. However, you should not rush your reading as you might miss some important information.

In 10 minutes, you should aim to:
- read the text carefully
- read the questions
- read the text again with the questions in mind.

The questions will usually be as follows:

Q A1	5 marks	You will have to find five details in the first part of the text and list them.
Q A2	5 marks	This is a language question. You will generally be asked how the writer uses language for a particular purpose, such as to establish character, in a section of the text.
Q A3	10 marks	This question will either be another language question, or a question asking you what impression you receive of a particular character, place or event in the extract.
Q A4	10 marks	Depending on what you were asked in Question 3, Question 4 will either ask you a language question or what impression you receive of a character, place or event in the extract. For example, if you are asked a language question in Question 3, you will be asked what impression you receive of something in the text for Question 4.
Q A5	10 marks	This question will either ask you to evaluate the way someone or something is presented in the text or whether you agree with a statement about the text.

To answer Question A1, you just need to find and list points in order to answer and you do not have to use your own words, although you can if you wish.

For the other questions, you will be asked to 'refer to the language used' or 'use evidence from the text to support your answer'. This means that you will be expected to make points, support them with evidence from the text and explain your ideas.

There are no marks for spelling, sentence construction or punctuation in this section, but you should still express yourself clearly.

Using textual references

REVISED

What this skill involves

You will be expected to support your ideas in Section A on both components. These can be quotes – direct words and phrases copied directly from the text – or a general reference to the characters and events, or an account of an activity that you put into your own words.

Question 1 on each paper is slightly different as you will be asked to list information that you have found, or find a short, relatively straightforward answer from the text.

For questions that ask you *how* a writer creates a certain impression or to *evaluate* the presentation of a character, place or experience, you will need to choose references that support the point you are making.

This means that you will need to:
● find key words and phrases to answer the question
● use inverted commas around direct quotes.

What the examiner is looking for

The mark scheme says that you need to draw **inferences** and justify these with evidence. This means that you need to use the ideas in the text to work out ideas about characters, events or experiences that the writer hasn't directly stated, then find textual references to back up what you have inferred (worked out).

> **inference**: using the clues in the text to work out something that the writer doesn't directly tell you

In this unit you will revise:
● how to use direct quotation
● how to paraphrase information.

Using evidence

REVISED

Point – **E**vidence – **E**xplanation is a useful technique that you can use when answering questions that ask you to:
● **analyse** language and structure
● **evaluate** a text
● **compare** two texts.

For these questions, you will need to find evidence to support your answer. The question will usually remind you of this, and might say: 'refer to the language used in the text to support your answer, using relevant subject terminology'.

You need to read the question carefully, then:
● make your **Point**
● find **Evidence** to support your idea
● **Explain** what this evidence shows.

Note how many marks your question is worth. Your examiner is not counting your quotes and is more interested in the quality of what you write, but as a guide, a 5-mark question would need **P**oint – **E**vidence – **E**xplanation completed about three times. A 10-mark question would need **P**oint – **E**vidence – **E**xplanation completed five or six times. Just copying out six quotes will not earn you 6 out of 10 as you would lack **points** and **explanations**. Remember to follow the structure.

Exam tip

To avoid repetition in your answer, you should use a range of phrases to build your **P**oint – **E**vidence – **E**xplanation structure.

Point	Evidence	Explanation
The writer: ● describes ● illustrates ● presents.	Quotations should be: ● relevant ● short ● in inverted commas.	This conveys This implies This portrays This suggests.

Making evidence precise

The best textual references are well selected and purposeful. This means that they are as precise as possible and support your point. Direct quotes should be individual words or short phrases. If you copy out big chunks of text you are not being selective enough.

Task

Read the beginning of the following story. Consider the question:

1 What do you learn about the character of Hale?   (5 marks)

> Hale knew, before he had been in Brighton three hours, that they meant to murder him. With his inky fingers and his bitten nails, his manner cynical and nervous, anybody could tell he didn't belong – belong to the early summer sun, the cool Whitsun wind off the sea, the holiday crowd. They came in by train from Victoria every five minutes, rocked down Queen's Road standing on the tops of the little local trams, stepped off in bewildered multitudes into fresh and glittering air: the new silver paint sparkled on the piers, the cream houses ran away into the west like a pale Victorian watercolour; a race in miniature motors, a band playing, flower gardens in bloom below the front, an aeroplane advertising something for the health in pale vanishing clouds across the sky.
>
> It had seemed quite easy to Hale to be lost in Brighton. Fifty thousand people besides himself were down for the day, and for quite a while he gave himself up to the good day.

(*Brighton Rock*, Graham Greene, 1938)

A student has selected three references that they could use in their answer:
● 'Hale knew, before he had been in Brighton three hours, that they meant to murder him'
● 'With his inky fingers and his bitten nails, his manner cynical and nervous'
● '… anybody could tell he didn't belong – belong to the early summer sun'

The selected references are all relevant to the answer, but are rather long. Aim to reduce each one to a short phrase that you could use instead of the whole quote. You may find that more than one phrase could be taken from some of the sentences.

Now try answering the question, using your short references instead of the student's long ones.

Tasks

Now read the extract again. Consider the question:

How does the writer present the setting in this extract?   (5 marks)

1 Consider three or four pieces of evidence that you could use in your answer.
2 Now see if you could make these selections shorter, by reducing them to a key phrase, or even to just one word.
   For example:
   ○ The 'stepped off in bewildered multitudes into fresh and glittering air' can be reduced to 'fresh and glittering'
   ○ The 'the new silver paint sparkled on the piers' can be reduced to 'new' and 'sparkled'.
3 Consider what these references show you about the setting. For example: 'new' and 'sparkled' suggest that the town is well maintained.

Embedding quotations

Embedding short quotations into your answer will help to make your responses even more purposeful. You will still be using a **P**oint – **E**vidence – **E**xplanation structure, but an embedded quotation is part of your sentence rather than standing alone.

For example: 'The fact that the pier "sparkled" with "new" paint suggests that the town is well maintained. It sounds like a bright and uplifting place here.'

Task

Read the following non-fiction extract about the awful conditions in Victorian schools for the children of prisoners.

> The children in these schools are enough to break the heart and hope of any man. I have never taken a foreigner or a stranger of any kind to one of these establishments but I have seen him so moved at sight of the child offenders, that he has been little able to disguise his emotion.
>
> (*The Daily News*, letter written by Charles Dickens, 4 February 1846)

1 What impression does the writer create of these schools?
   To practise embedding quotations, choose three short pieces of evidence that you could use to prove that these schools seem awful places. For example: 'break the heart'.
   Now try to embed each quote into a **P**oint – **E**vidence – **E**xplanation structure that is part of your sentence. For example: 'The fact that a visit to one of these schools would "break the heart" illustrates how shocking they are.'

Paraphrasing evidence

When you **paraphrase** information from the text, you use your own words. This is not a simple skill. To do this well, you need to be able to put what the writer said into different words but keep the same meaning. This proves to the examiner that you understand the text because, after all, if you can't put it into your own words, you probably don't understand it.

> **paraphrase**: to put something into your own words but keep the same meaning

Tasks

Read the following short extract about a girl who has been dared to visit an abandoned house.

> The gravel drive was short but still served to cut the house off from the rest of the street. I took a few tentative steps away from the warm glow of the streetlamps, until I was inside the gate and, technically, now on private land. Each slow step towards the house was met with a crunch of gravel underfoot, and although I knew that the place had been abandoned for years, my echoing footsteps signalled more about my arrival than I would have liked. I was not just aware of the speeding thump of my heart, but also of my skin prickling, my tongue seeming to dry out and even my blood coursing through my veins. This had been a stupid idea.

Exam tip

When you paraphrase, you do not have to replace *every* word in the original text with a different one or your words. This can end up sounding silly.

Read the four quotes below that have been taken from the above extract and write a paraphrased statement for each. One has been done for you.

1 'served to cut the house off from the rest of the street' – the house stands alone, separated from other buildings
2 'away from the warm glow of the streetlamps'
3 'met with a crunch of gravel underfoot'
4 'signalled more about my arrival than I would have liked'

Exam tip

When answering the longer 'how' questions, aim to use a variety of quotations and some paraphrasing to show the examiner that you are capable of both skills.

Task

Re-read the previous extract about an abandoned house. A student has answered the following question:

How does the writer show that she is scared?   (10 marks)

1 Based on the table below, what grade might it have been awarded?
  Check:
  ○ whether all the points made answer the question
  ○ whether all the quotes are relevant.

the explanation only partly supports the point being made

accurate use of paraphrase

Point – **E**vidence – **E**xplanation structure is used well here

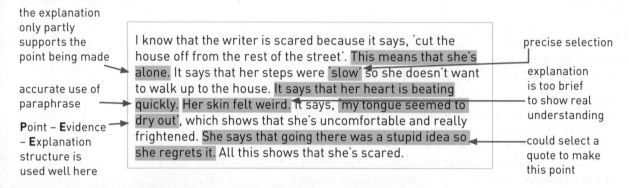

I know that the writer is scared because it says, 'cut the house off from the rest of the street'. This means that she's alone. It says that her steps were 'slow' so she doesn't want to walk up to the house. It says that her heart is beating quickly. Her skin felt weird. It says, 'my tongue seemed to dry out', which shows that she's uncomfortable and really frightened. She says that going there was a stupid idea so she regrets it. All this shows that she's scared.

precise selection

explanation is too brief to show real understanding

could select a quote to make this point

Grades	Descriptors
9	Insightful analysis of the way the writer presents fear.
7, 8	Draws inferences and justifies these with precise evidence.
5, 6	Uses a range of well-chosen evidence to support accurate comments.
4	Uses appropriate references and begins to analyse the writer's fear.
3	Explains what happens. Simple references.
1, 2	Begins to comment on some general impressions.

Assessment comment

Grade 4. The response answers the question, finds appropriate references and begins to analyse how the writer shows that she is scared. It is a correct but short answer. The phrase 'It says' is a bit repetitive.

Test yourself

TESTED ☐

Read the following extract and answer the question:

How does the writer convey the impression that teaching is a dangerous job?   (5 marks)

Nearly half of exclusions – 44.3 per cent – were the result of attacks on other pupils and teachers. Some 530 pupils were excluded as a result of violence against an adult, at a time when teachers say they feel increasingly unsafe in classrooms. Other pupils were sent home from school for verbal and racial abuse, misconduct and persistent disruptive behaviour.

(Extract from *Daily Mail* article, 31 March 2016)

Aim for:
● short references
● paraphrased evidence
● embedded quotation.

Answers on p. 97

How to prepare for the exam

Read a review of a film in a newspaper or online. Look for words and phrases that show you the reviewer liked or disliked it. Pick out individual words that give you this impression.

Component 1, QA1 Extracting key information

What this question involves

You will have to list five points that you have found in the opening section of the extract. You could be asked, for example, to find five details about a character, setting or event.

This question tests the ability to identify explicit and implicit information and ideas. This means that ideas may be clearly stated (explicit information) or you may have to work out what is implied in the text (implicit).

Your aim is to make a simple list. You do not need to analyse the writer's language choices in this question and will be wasting time if you do.

Timing

You will already have read the extract. There are 5 marks for this question, so aim to spend about 5 minutes answering it.

What the examiner is looking for

The examiner is looking for evidence that you can:
- select the right details from the text
- make a clear list of these details.

You can put your ideas into your own words or quote directly from the text. Note that no marks will be given for unabridged quotation of whole sentences. This means that you can't copy big chunks of the extract out.

In this unit you will revise:
- how to find and use relevant information from the text.

Extracting key information

Remember that the information can be both **explicit** and **implicit**. There will be short details that you can just copy out, and other ideas that you will need to think about more in order to work out what they are really saying. You then need to think of a clear way of expressing these.

> **explicit information**: clearly stated – leaving no doubt
>
> **implicit information**: an implied or suggested idea

Task

Read lines 1–11.

> What we saw when we stood from our picnic was this: a huge grey balloon, the size of a house, the shape of a teardrop, had come down in the field. The pilot must have been halfway out of the passenger basket as it touched the ground. His leg had become entangled in a rope that
> 5 was attached to an anchor. Now, as the wind gusted and pushed and lifted the balloon toward the escarpment, he was being half dragged, half carried across the field. In the basket was a child, a boy of about ten. In a sudden lull, the man was on his feet, clutching at the basket, or at the boy. Then there was another gust, and the pilot was on his back,
> 10 bumping over the rough ground, trying to dig his feet in for purchase or lunging for the anchor behind him in order to secure it in the earth.
>
> As I ran I heard him shouting at the boy, urging him to leap clear of the basket. But the boy was tossed from one side to another as the balloon lurched across the field. He regained his balance and got a leg

15 over the edge of the basket. The balloon rose and fell, thumping into a hummock, and the boy dropped backward out of sight. Then he was up again, arms stretched out toward the man and shouting something in return – words or inarticulate fear, I couldn't tell.

(*Enduring Love*, Ian McEwan, 1997)

1 Which five details about the pilot could you use in an answer?
  a He was halfway out of the basket.
  b His leg was tangled in a rope.
  c He had lost control of the balloon.
  d There was a child in the basket of the balloon.
  e The wind knocked the pilot on to his back.
  f He was shouting at the boy.
  g The wind was blowing the balloon across the ground.
  h He made lots of attempts to stop the balloon.

Typical mistakes

For this type of 'list' question, you should not explain your answer or analyse the language used. You will not lose marks for this but you will not be credited for it.

Mark scheme

You will be awarded 1 mark for each correct point, up to a maximum of 5.

The answers are **a**, **b**, **c**, **e**, **h**.

Statements **d** and **g** are not about the pilot and Statement **f** is after line 11 so is outside the line references given.

To help you identify different types of ideas, now decide which of the five details that you chose are explicit information and which are implicit.

Answers **a, b** and **e** are explicit information.

Answers **c** and **h** are implicit information.

Exam tip

Read the question carefully, then look only at the line references given. Highlight details that you think are relevant. If you have more than five, decide which are the best.

Test yourself

TESTED

Read the extract. List five things that you learn about Mr Bellingham.

The cloakroom was crowded with boys, jostling in the cramped space as they pulled on shorts, or jumped about on one foot, fumbling with knotted laces. Mr Bellingham, a bull-necked, white-haired man in his fifties, stood on the doorway, speaking sharply to any boy who appeared to be loitering.

The double swing doors burst open, and Colin Harper skidded to a halt.

'Late again, Harper?'

'I had to see Mr Sawdon, Sir.'

'What about?'

'Being late, Sir.'

Mr Bellingham closed his eyes. 'Why did I ask that?' He opened them again. 'Well, go on then, get ready. Don't just stand there.' Raising his voice, he turned to the rest of the class. 'Lesson'll be over before some of you lot get started.'

(*The Man Who Wasn't There*, Pat Barker, 1989)

Answers on p. 97

How to prepare for the exam

Read the opening paragraph of a chapter from a book. Find five things that you learn about the character, setting or events.

Component 1, QA2 Writing about language

What this question involves

You will usually be asked how the writer shows you something about a character, setting or event in a particular part of the extract. The key word here is *how*.

This means that you will need to:
- find key words and phrases to answer the question
- understand why the writer has chosen these words
- explain the effect of the words clearly and effectively.

This question is worth 5 marks.

Timing

You will already have read the extract. There are 5 marks for this question and you need to spend some time explaining the effect of the language, so aim to spend about 6 minutes answering it.

What the examiner is looking for

The examiner is looking for evidence that you can:
- analyse how writers use language and structure
- support what you say with relevant quotations
- use subject terminology where appropriate.

Using subject terminology means that you should try to write the correct word for a particular technique (such as simile, metaphor, alliteration, personification) or word class (such as **nouns**, **verbs**, **adverbs** and **adjectives**).

In this unit you will revise:
- how to find specific techniques
- how to use subject terminology with confidence.

Tasks

Read the following extract. In this passage, one brother is attempting to climb under a bridge to show off after an argument.

Consider the question:

How does the writer make this extract dramatic?

> 'Arthur!' – his voice a shriek – 'I'm going to fall.'
>
> 'Good,' Arthur said.
>
> The word that would haunt him for the rest of his life. He felt Jake fall. Felt the weight leave the bridge. Just like that. For a moment, Arthur was paralysed. He couldn't even draw breath. Then his breath came with a rush and he grabbed the rail and looked over. He expected Jake to be washed downstream but, in fact, he was under the bridge, face up, motionless, wedged between two rocks. Water was streaming around him. Over his face.
>
> Arthur didn't remember afterwards how he got to the river. He must have slid down the bank or jumped. He waded into the icy surge, the breath knocked out of him by the cold. He wondered if this was another

noun: naming word; these can be concrete nouns that identify something you can see (boy, teacher, office) or abstract nouns that name a quality or state (courage, fear, love)

verb: an action telling us what a person or thing does (scream, leap, discover), an event (rain, happen) or a situation (be, have)

adverb: gives more information about an action (she shouted loudly, he nearly cried)

adjective: describes the noun (a strict teacher, the spacious office, pure fear, true love)

trick, if Jake was playing dead for fun. One further, final joke. But Jake's head lolled to one side, and the water streamed out of his nose and mouth in a way that made Arthur cry out in fear.

The bank was too steep to climb so he waded along the edge of the river, the water boiling around him, stumbling over rocks, feet and legs numb. He carried Jake in his arms and then, once he found a way up, he slung him over his shoulder. He thought he was alive but he couldn't be sure. And who knew what further injuries he, Arthur, might cause by heaving him over his shoulder. But what else could he do?

At the top, he lowered Jake carefully to the ground to check that he was breathing, and he was, so he picked him up again and ran.

(*The Other Side of the Bridge*, Mary Lawson, 2007)

1 Pick out two adjectives, two verbs and an adverb, which help to make this extract dramatic.

2 How does the writer make this extract dramatic?

> **Exam tip**
>
> Remember that finding these words is only the first step of your answer. You must comment on their effect to earn marks.

Mark scheme

Grade	Descriptors
9	Insightful comments about a wide range of dramatic events and precise analysis of how language achieves effects. Careful use of subject terminology to support comments, such as the dramatic verbs used when Jake is drowning and the contrast in the adverb 'carefully' when Arthur places Jake on the floor.
7, 8	Accurate and perceptive comments about the dramatic events, supported by purposeful examples. Analyses how language is used to achieve effects. Subject terminology is used accurately, such as the exciting verbs when Arthur 'grabbed' the rail and 'waded' into the water, or use of adjectives, such as Jake being 'motionless'.
5, 6	Explores the drama in these lines. Some thoughtful analysis of how language is used to achieve effects with well-chosen evidence to support.
4	Comments on the drama. Supports with relevant examples. Starts to look at how language is used to achieve effects.
3	States what happens. Straightforward textual references. May make simple comments on the writer's choice of words.
1, 2	Comments on some general impressions. May find some simple examples.

The response below demonstrates Grade 9 skills in response to question 2 above.

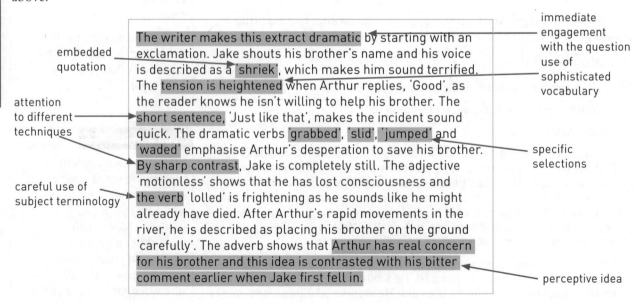

embedded quotation

immediate engagement with the question

use of sophisticated vocabulary

attention to different techniques

careful use of subject terminology

specific selections

perceptive idea

The writer makes this extract dramatic by starting with an exclamation. Jake shouts his brother's name and his voice is described as a 'shriek', which makes him sound terrified. The tension is heightened when Arthur replies, 'Good', as the reader knows he isn't willing to help his brother. The short sentence, 'Just like that', makes the incident sound quick. The dramatic verbs 'grabbed', 'slid', 'jumped' and 'waded' emphasise Arthur's desperation to save his brother. By sharp contrast, Jake is completely still. The adjective 'motionless' shows that he has lost consciousness and the verb 'lolled' is frightening as he sounds like he might already have died. After Arthur's rapid movements in the river, he is described as placing his brother on the ground 'carefully'. The adverb shows that Arthur has real concern for his brother and this idea is contrasted with his bitter comment earlier when Jake first fell in.

Tasks

1 Read the following extracts from the Roald Dahl story 'The Hitchhiker'. In each extract, find the technique stated. Comment on its effect.

   a Simile:

   He was a small ratty-faced man with grey teeth. His eyes were dark and quick and clever, like rats' eyes, and his ears were slightly pointed at the top.

   b Metaphor:

   I had a new car. It was an exciting toy; a big BMW 3.3 Li, which means 3.3 litre, long wheelbase, fuel injection.

   c Personification:

   The powerful engine growled and grunted impatiently at slow speeds, but at sixty miles an hour the growling stopped and the motor began to purr with pleasure.

   d Alliteration:

   'I'm goin' right through London and out the other side' he said. 'I'm goin' to Epsom, for the races. It's Derby Day today.'

   'So it is,' I said. 'I wish I were going with you. I love betting on horses.'

   'I never bet on horses,' he said. 'I don't even watch 'em run. That's a stupid silly business.'

   'Then why do you go?' I asked.

   He didn't seem to like that question. His little ratty face went absolutely blank and he sat there staring straight ahead at the road, saying nothing.

Answers:

   a 'His eyes were ... like rats' eyes' – makes him sound cunning.

   b 'It was an exciting toy' – the owner is delighted with the car; 'toy' suggests he might drive it recklessly.

   c 'growled', 'grunted', 'purr' – it sounds alive / like it has a personality.

   d Arguably, 'Derby Day' (although this is its name), 'stupid silly' emphasises his opinion; 'sat there staring straight' – sounds a little sinister.

2 What techniques can you find in these quotations from the same story?

   a Like an executioner approaching his victim, the cop came strolling slowly toward us.

   b The belt had a brass buckle of beautiful design.

   c We sat there like guilty schoolboys, waiting for him to arrive, 'Watch out for this man,' my passenger whispered, 'He looks mean as the devil.'

   d He nodded, watching me all the time with his black rat's eyes.

   e 'We'd better build a little bonfire and burn these books.'

   f They looked more like the fingers of a brain surgeon or a watchmaker.

Answers:

a simile	**b** alliteration	**c** similes
d metaphor	**e** alliteration	**f** simile

simile: a comparison using 'like' or 'as' ('as slippery as polished ice')

metaphor: a comparison which says something or someone is something else ('the branches were fingers')

personification: when a thing, an idea or an animal is given human attributes ('the cold water bit at his ankles')

alliteration: when a series of words in a row (or close to a row) have the same first consonant sound ('the crows called crisply to each other')

3 Choose any three of the above quotes that tell you something about character. Write a short response, explaining what they tell you. Use correct subject terminology.

For example: 'We learn that one of the men sounds cunning, when the narrator says that the man watched him with, "his black rat's eyes". A rat is associated with being untrustworthy or sly, so this metaphor shows that the narrator feels uneasy.'

4 Now read this longer extract from 'The Hitchhiker'. In this part of the story, a driver and his passenger – a hitchhiker – have been caught speeding. Practise finding evidence for a 5-mark 'how' question by picking out three or four short quotes that you could use to answer the question:

How does the writer present the policeman in these lines?   (5 marks)

You must refer to the language used in the text to support your answer, using relevant subject terminology.

> The cop got off his motorcycle and leaned the machine sideways onto its prop stand. Then he took off his gloves and placed them carefully on the seat. He was in no hurry now. He had us where he wanted us and he knew it.
>
> 'This is real trouble,' I said. 'I don't like it one little bit.'
>
> 'Don't talk to 'im more than is necessary, you understand,' my companion said. 'Just sit tight and keep mum.'
>
> Like an executioner approaching his victim, the cop came strolling slowly toward us. He was a big meaty man with a belly, and his blue breeches were skin-tight around his enormous thighs. His goggles were pulled up on the helmet, showing a smouldering red face with wide cheeks.
>
> We sat there like guilty schoolboys, waiting for him to arrive.
>
> 'Watch out for this man,' my passenger whispered, ''E looks mean as the devil.'
>
> The cop came round to my open window and placed one meaty hand on the sill.
>
> 'What's the hurry?' he said.
>
> 'No hurry, officer,' I answered.
>
> 'Perhaps there's a woman in the back having a baby and you're rushing her to hospital? Is that it?'
>
> 'No, officer.'
>
> 'Or perhaps your house is on fire and you're dashing home to rescue the family from upstairs?' His voice was dangerously soft and mocking.

5 Once you have selected your evidence, write your answer to the question. In your answer, try to use some of the subject terminology that you have just revised.

This is what a Grade 5 student wrote about the language:

> The policeman sounds like an unpleasant person. He's obviously enjoying making the men wait to be questioned. He put his gloves 'carefully on the seat', which shows that he's not in any hurry. A simile is used when it says, 'Like an executioner approaching his victim' which makes the policeman sound dangerous. He also sounds dangerous when it says that he was 'a big meaty man' because you wouldn't want to argue with someone like that. When he questions the men, his voice is described as 'soft and mocking', which makes him sound nasty.

This is a Grade 8 response:

> The policeman is presented as enjoying the moment when he's caught the driver speeding. He is described as being 'in no hurry' as he makes the most of the moment before questioning the driver. He sounds threatening in the simile 'Like an executioner approaching his victim' and the reader receives the impression that he is going to deal with the driver severely. The adjectives 'meaty', 'enormous' and 'wide' make him sound huge and intimidating. His 'smouldering' face also suggests that he is angry. The hitchhiker observes that the policeman looks 'mean as the devil' and this simile suggests that he is an evil and spiteful man. The policeman is sarcastic as he suggests unlikely reasons for the driver speeding. He knows that these reasons are not why the driver was going too fast, but he asks him anyway because he's enjoying his discomfort.

Typical mistakes

Do not just find techniques. Writing that 'a verb is used' will not earn you marks. You need to look at the effect created by the writer's use of this verb.

Assessment comment

The Grade 5 response explains the effect of a variety of techniques and uses relevant quotations. It makes accurate and thoughtful points. The Grade 8 response has more of a range of points and more specific selections from the text. The student's comments are perceptive because they are using more inference to work out what the policeman is like from the way he speaks and behaves.

Exam tip

One way to make your references precise is to look for specific techniques and word classes that can help you to answer the question.

Exam tip

The writer has thought carefully about choosing the exact words they need in order to create a particular impression of a character, event or setting, so you should look closely at their vocabulary.

Test yourself

Read the following extract. It gives an account of a hot air balloon that is out of control, with a ten-year-old boy stuck in the basket beneath and the pilot tangled in the balloon's rope. A group of men are trying to stop the balloon from taking off again.

Consider the following question and read the extract below:

How does the writer make this extract dramatic? (5 marks)

> The wind renewed its rage in the treetops just before I felt its force on my back. Then it struck the balloon, which ceased its innocent, comical wagging and was suddenly stilled. Its only motion was a shimmer of strain that rippled out across its ridged surface as the contained energy accumulated. It broke free, the anchor flew up in a spray of dirt, and balloon and basket rose ten feet in the air. The boy was thrown back, out of sight. The pilot had the rope in his hands and was lifted two feet clear off the ground. If Logan had not reached him and taken hold of one of the many dangling lines, the balloon would have carried the boy away. Instead, both men were now being pulled across the field, and the farmworkers and I were running again.
>
> I got there before them. When I took a rope, the basket was above head height. The boy inside it was screaming. Despite the wind, I caught the smell of urine. Jed Parry was on a rope seconds after me, and the two farmworkers, Joseph Lacey and Toby Greene, caught hold just after him. Greene was having a coughing fit, but he kept his grip. The pilot was shouting instructions at us, but too frantically, and no one was listening. He had been struggling too long, and now he was exhausted and emotionally out of control.
>
> (*Enduring Love*, Ian McEwan, 1997)

1 Pick out two adjectives, two verbs, an adverb, alliteration and personification which help to make these lines dramatic. Remember to comment on the effect of these techniques in order to earn marks.
2 Now write a full answer for the question: How does the writer make this extract dramatic?

Answers on p. 97–98

How to prepare for the exam

Select two paragraphs to read of a short story or novel. Find four or five words or phrases that make this part of the story interesting. Think of the subject terminology that you would use to comment on these.

Component 1, QA3 Creating an impression

Component 1 Question A3 may ask you 'what impression' you receive of a character, place or event in the text. Alternatively, Question 3 may ask you how the writer shows you something and the 'what impression' question will be Question 4 instead. This unit will look at how a writer creates an impression.

What this question involves

You are likely to be asked what impression you receive of a person, place or event in the text. This is similar to a 'how' question, as you will be looking at the language choices the writer makes in order to create this impression, and what a character says or does that helps you see them in a certain way. You will be reminded to refer to the text for your answer and to use subject terminology.

This question is worth 10 marks.

Timing

You will already have read the extract, although you will need to re-read the specific lines that the question directs you to, and keep the question in mind as you read these lines. There are 10 marks for this question and you need to state clearly what your impression is and also explain the effect of the language that encourages you to hold this impression, so aim to spend about 12 minutes answering.

What the examiner is looking for

The examiner is looking for evidence that you can:
- understand what **impression** is being created of a person, place or event
- analyse how the writer creates these impressions
- use relevant subject terminology to support your views.

In this unit you will revise:
- how language choices help us to form an impression
- how to analyse these language choices.

> **impression**: an opinion or a feeling that you have about a character from the way they speak and behave and the language used to describe them

Impressions of character

REVISED

Tasks

1 Read this description of character. What impressions do you receive of Tom in these lines? (10 marks)

Tom Buchanan in riding clothes was standing with his legs apart on the front porch.

He had changed since his New Haven years. Now he was a sturdy straw-haired man of thirty with a rather hard mouth and a supercilious manner. Two shining arrogant eyes had established dominance over his face and gave him the appearance of always leaning aggressively forward. Not even the effeminate swank of his riding clothes could hide the enormous power of that body – he seemed to fill those glistening boots until he strained the top lacing, and you could see a great pack of muscle shifting when his shoulder moved under his thin coat. It was a body capable of enormous leverage – a cruel body.

His speaking voice, a gruff husky tenor, added to the impression of fractiousness he conveyed. There was a touch of paternal contempt in it, even toward people he liked – and there were men at New Haven who had hated his guts.

(*The Great Gatsby*, F. Scott Fitzgerald, 1925)

2 What do each of the following quotations suggest about Tom?
  a 'was standing with his legs apart on the front porch'
  b 'a rather hard mouth and a supercilious manner'
  c 'Two shining arrogant eyes'
  d 'the appearance of always leaning aggressively forward'
  e 'the enormous power of that body'
Continue this response by using two more of the selected quotes to say what impressions you receive of Tom.

comments on impression of character

makes deductions about character

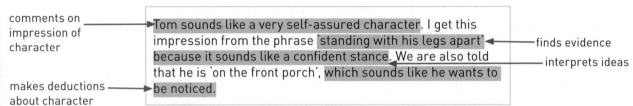

finds evidence

interprets ideas

Tom sounds like a very self-assured character. I get this impression from the phrase 'standing with his legs apart' because it sounds like a confident stance. We are also told that he is 'on the front porch', which sounds like he wants to be noticed.

3 Now extend this response by using the rest of the extract to say what further impressions you receive of Tom.

Task

Read this description of a character called Myrtle Wilson, which occurs later in the novel, *The Great Gatsby*.

I heard footsteps on the stairs, and in a moment the thickish figure of a woman blocked out the light from the office door. She was in the middle thirties, and faintly stout, but she carried her flesh sensuously as some women can. Her face, above a spotted dress of dark blue crêpe-de-chine, contained no facet or gleam of beauty, but there was an immediate perceptible vitality about her as if the nerves of her body were continually smouldering. She smiled slowly and, walking through her husband as if he were a ghost, shook hands with Tom, looking him flush in the eye. Then she wet her lips, and without turning around spoke to her husband in a soft, coarse voice: 'Get some chairs, why don't you, so somebody can sit down.'

(*The Great Gatsby*, F. Scott Fitzgerald, 1925)

1 What impressions of Myrtle do we receive here? Comment on:
  a how she is made to sound attractive
  b her attitude towards her husband
  c how you can tell that she is attracted to Tom.
  Answers:
  a How she is made to sound attractive – 'carried her flesh sensuously', 'an immediate perceptible vitality', 'continually smouldering', 'soft' voice.
  b Her attitude towards her husband – 'walking through her husband as if he were a ghost', 'without turning around spoke to her husband', 'Get some chairs, why don't you'.
  c How you can tell that she is attracted to Tom – 'smiled slowly', ignores her husband, 'shook hands with Tom', 'looking him flush in the eye', 'wet her lips'.

Exam tip

Top-grade students have a sense of **overview** in their answers. This means that they analyse details but also look at how these contribute to our impressions of a character as a whole. When you write about character, try to comment on the overall impression that you receive at the end of the extract.

overview: the 'bigger picture' or summary of the text

Typical mistakes

Although you are likely to be asked what impression you receive of a character, do not be tempted to give too personal a response. You can say, for example, that they seem arrogant or unkind, but not whether you know anyone like this or how you would act if you met this sort of character.

Impressions of relationships

Tasks

The previous question asked you to look at Myrtle Wilson's attitude towards her husband and her attraction towards another man, Tom. You will have seen that her relationship with her husband is a negative one, as she virtually ignores him, while she flirts with Tom. A question may ask you to look at the relationships between characters or their attitudes towards each other.

Read the following extract. In these lines, Myrtle's sister, Catherine, asks her why she married a man she doesn't love.

> 'Why did you, Myrtle?' demanded Catherine. 'Nobody forced you to.'
>
> Myrtle considered.
>
> 'I married him because I thought he was a gentleman,' she said finally. 'I thought he knew something about breeding, but he wasn't fit to lick my shoe.'
>
> 'You were crazy about him for a while,' said Catherine.
>
> 'Crazy about him!' cried Myrtle incredulously. 'Who said I was crazy about him? I never was any more crazy about him than I was about that man there.'
>
> She pointed suddenly at me, and everyone looked at me accusingly. I tried to show by my expression that I expected no affection.
>
> 'The only crazy I was was when I married him. I knew right away I made a mistake. He borrowed somebody's best suit to get married in, and never even told me about it, and the man came after it one day when he was out: "Oh, is that your suit?" I said. "This is the first I ever heard about it." But I gave it to him and then I lay down and cried.'
>
> (*The Great Gatsby*, F. Scott Fitzgerald, 1925)

1 What impression do you get of Myrtle's attitude towards her husband?
2 Finish each of these **P**oint – **E**vidence – **E**xplanation structures by saying what Myrtle's attitude towards her husband is.
   a Myrtle struggles to explain why she married her husband, shown by the phrases, 'Myrtle considered' and 'she said finally'. This suggests that …
   b Myrtle's attitude is shown in the comment, 'he wasn't fit to lick my shoe', showing that she thinks …
   c Her exclamation 'Crazy about him!' conveys …
   d She calls their marriage 'a mistake', suggesting that …
   e Myrtle is very derogatory about her husband, making her seem quite a harsh character. Our opinion of her slightly changes, however, when she says, 'I lay down and cried' because …

To develop your response even further, you can try adding to your explanations by focusing in on a specific part of the quotation and analysing the effect of the language used. By doing this, you will be undertaking specific language analysis, which is a high-grade skill. If you can also use relevant subject terminology, you can improve your answer even more.

3 Look at the example below, where a **P**oint – **E**vidence – **E**xplanation structure has been used first, then the **E**xplanation has been added to with specific language analysis and use of subject terminology. Practise this technique yourself with the quotation below:

> 'I married him because I thought he was a gentleman,' she said finally.

sentence 1 uses a **P**oint – **E**vidence – **E**xplanation structure

specific language analysis

The exclamation, '"Crazy about him!" cried Myrtle incredulously' conveys that Myrtle strongly disagrees with her sister's suggestion. The adverb 'incredulously' shows that she is amazed that anyone would think that she ever loved her husband, which further emphasises her dislike of him.

precise selection

subject terminology

the response is developed further by a second sentence

Impressions of place

REVISED

A writer aims to transport their readers to the places they describe in their story. In order to create a sense of place, they may use precise descriptions and details. You should also consider the way a character reacts to their setting and what emotions they feel when they are there.

Tasks

Look closely at this description of the town of Struan in Ontario, Canada. As you read, consider the question:

What impression of Struan is created in this extract? (10 marks)

> What was Struan, apart from a sawmill? A sorry bunch of stores lined up along a dusty main street, with nothing in them anyone would want to buy. A couple of churches. The Hudson's Bay Company. A post office. A bank. Harper's Restaurant. Ben's Bar. A hotel – because, incredibly, some people chose to come to Struan for their vacations – and a little clutch of holiday cottages down by the lake. The lake was the town's only asset, in Ian's opinion. It was large – fifty miles long, north to south, and almost twenty miles across – and deep, and very clear, surrounded on all sides by low granite hills studded with spruce and wind-blasted pines. Its shore was so ragged with bays and inlets and islands that you could spend your life exploring and never find half of them. When Ian dreamed of leaving the town, which he did all the time nowadays, the thought of leaving the lake was the only thing that bothered him.

(*The Other Side of the Bridge*, Mary Lawson, 2007)

Think about how you would answer this question by considering what you would write for each of the ideas below.
1 State what your overall impression of Struan is.
2 Consider the structure of the piece. Look at the effect of:
   a the question to start
   b the use of short sentences.
3 Consider the language choices. Look at:
   a adjectives
   b verbs
   c use of facts.
4 Look at the character's reaction to this place.

If you wrote about each of these aspects, you could write a thorough answer to the question.

A Grade 8 student has used the above plan to write the following response to the same question.

overall impression →

Struan is presented as a small, uninspiring town at first. The use of a question to start makes it sound as if the writer is struggling to think of anything interesting to say about the place where he lives. The use of short sentences to describe the different parts of the town makes it sound boring. The writer says there is 'A post office. A bank.' He doesn't describe them, which suggests there is nothing else to say. He uses the adjective 'sorry' to describe the shops, and says that there is 'nothing in them anyone would want to buy', which makes them sound pointless. He is also amazed that anyone would ever want to come there on holiday and that, 'incredibly', there was a hotel, which he can hardly believe.

However, he is more positive in the rest of the extract. He uses the adjectives 'deep' and 'clear' to describe the lake. He uses impressive facts, saying that it is 'fifty miles long' and explains that 'you could spend your life exploring' the bays around it. This makes it sound mysterious and tempting. He makes the area sound beautiful and natural by describing the 'low granite hills studded with spruce and wind-blasted pines'. The scenery sounds stunning. The verb 'dreamed' shows that he has fantasised about leaving, but the lake draws him back. We finish with a different impression of Struan than we had at the start of the extract.

→ considers structure

→ analyses language choices

→ looks at the writer's reaction

uses subject terminology →

→ considers a range of techniques

→ detail

→ ends with a point about structure

considers technique →

Tasks

Look closely at the following extract which describes the town of Holcomb in Kansas. Consider the question:

What impression of Holcomb is created in this extract?   (10 marks)

> Holcomb can be seen from great distances. Not that there is much to see – simply an aimless congregation of buildings divided in the centre by the main-line tracks of the Santa Fe Railroad, a haphazard hamlet bounded on the south by a brown stretch of the Arkansas (pronounced 'Ar-kan-sas') River, on the north by a highway, route 50, and in the east and west by prairie lands and wheat fields. After rain, or when snowfalls thaw, the streets, unnamed, unshaded, unpaved, turn from the thickest dust into the direst mud. At one end of the town stands a stark old stucco structure, the roof of which supports an electric sign – DANCE – but the dancing has ceased and the advertisement has been dark for several years. Nearby is another building with an irrelevant sign, this one in flaking gold on a dirty window – HOLCOMB BANK. The bank failed in 1933, and its former counting rooms have been converted into apartments. It is one of the town's two 'apartment houses', the second being a ramshackle mansion known, because a good part of the local school's faculty lives there, as the Teacherage. But the majority of Holcomb's homes are one-storey frame affairs, with front porches.

(*In Cold Blood*, Truman Capote, 1965)

Answer the question by working through the following tasks.
1 State what your overall impression of Holcomb is.
2 Consider the structure of the piece. Look at the effect of:
   a starting by telling the reader that there is not much to see
   b the use of long sentences.

3 Consider the language choices. Look at:
  a adjectives
  b nouns
  c **superlatives**
  d use of facts.

4 Look at the sense of history evoked in this piece.

> **superlative**: this highest degree of something, such as 'best', 'most awful', 'ugliest', 'thinnest'

Mark scheme

Grade	Descriptors
9	Insightful comments about a wide range of impressions, supported by purposeful reference. Exacting analysis of the way Holcomb is presented through language and tone. Precise use of subject terminology.
7, 8	Perceptive comments on a range of details about Holcomb. Close analysis of how language and structure are used to achieve effects. Well-chosen subject terminology.
5, 6	Makes thoughtful comments about Holcomb, with reference to details. Analyses how language and structure are used to achieve effects. Subject terminology is used accurately.
4	Explains what it's like in Holcomb, with some understanding of how the writer uses language to achieve effects. Some use of relevant subject terminology.
3	States what Holcomb looks like. Straightforward textual references. May make simple comments on the writer's choice of words.
1, 2	Identifies and begins to comment on some simple aspects of Holcomb.

Impressions of events

REVISED ☐

To write about events, you will need to consider more than what takes place. Think about:

- what happens
- where it happens
- the characters' reactions to events.

Tasks

Read the following extract which gives an account of a fight between two ten-year-old boys.

Consider the question:

What impression do we get of the fight? How does the writer create this impression? (10 marks)

> I got my hand up to his hair; my hand was wet – his snot and tears. He couldn't let us separate: they'd see him crying. I tried to get his hands off and jump back – I couldn't. I kneed him – missed. He was squealing now, inside his mouth. I had his hair; I pulled his head back.
>
> – Cheating!
>
> Someone yelled that. I didn't care. It was stupid. This was the most important thing that had ever happened to me; I knew it.
>
> His head came into my face, mostly my mouth. There was blood – I could taste it.
>
> The pain was nice. It wasn't bad. It didn't matter. He did it again, not as good. He was pushing me back. If I fell it would be different. I went back – I was going. I fell back against someone. He got out of the way – jumped back – but it was too late; I'd got my feet steady again. This was great.

(*Paddy Clarke Ha Ha Ha*, Roddy Doyle, 1993)

1 Read the sample student response (below) to the given question. What advice would you give this student in order to improve the response?

> The fight is extremely violent. Both boys are taking it seriously. The writer struggles to move away from his opponent. He then tries to knee him. Someone shouts, 'Cheating!' but the writer doesn't care because he just wants to win. He says, 'This was the most important thing that had ever happened to me', which shows that he's determined to win. He starts bleeding. He actually seems to be enjoying the fight.

2 Has the student:
  a given an overall impression of the fight?
  b considered structure:
    i how the extract begins and ends?
    ii sentence length?
  c considered language:
    i verbs?
    ii adjectives?
    iii direct speech?
  d looked at the narrator's attitude towards the fight?

Test yourself

TESTED ☐

Read the following extract which gives an account of a girl who visits a psychiatrist.

Doctor Gordon twiddled a silver pencil.

'Your mother tells me you are upset.'

I curled in the cavernous leather chair and faced Doctor Gordon across an acre of highly polished desk.

Doctor Gordon waited. He tapped his pencil – tap, tap, tap – across the neat green field of his blotter.

His eyelashes were so long and thick they looked artificial. Black plastic reeds fringing two green, glacial pools.

Doctor Gordon's features were so perfect he was almost pretty.

I hated him the minute I walked through the door.

I had imagined a kindly, ugly, intuitive man looking up and saying, 'Ah!' in an encouraging way, as if he could see something I couldn't, and then I would find words to tell him how I was so scared, as if I were being stuffed farther and farther into a black, airless sack with no way out.

Then he would lean back in his chair and match the tips of his fingers together in a little steeple and tell me why I couldn't sleep and why I couldn't read and why I couldn't eat and why everything people did seemed so silly.

And then, I thought, he would help me, step by step, to be myself again.

But Doctor Gordon wasn't like that at all. He was young and good-looking, and I could see right away he was conceited.

(*The Bell Jar*, Sylvia Plath, 1963)

What impressions do you get of Doctor Gordon in this extract? (10 marks)

You must refer to the text to support your answer.

Answers on p. 98–99

How to prepare for the exam

An internet search of places from your favourite books or descriptions of settings will give you lots of opportunity to read about different settings. Think about what impression you receive of these places. Alternatively, put in a search for key phrases, such as 'a bustling city', or 'central New York', or 'the Yorkshire Moors'.

Component 1, QA4 Explaining language and structure

If Question 3 asked you, 'What impressions do you get of …', Question 4 is likely to be another 'how' question. For example, 'How does the writer show that the dog is frightened?', 'How does the writer show you what Grace and Annie think of each other?', 'How does the writer make these lines tense and dramatic for the reader?'

What this question involves

You are likely to be asked how the writer shows you something about a character, relationship, setting or event in a particular part of the extract. You will need to analyse how a writer uses language and **structure** to achieve effects.

This means that you will need to explain the effect of the writer's language choices, but also consider the structure of the extract – that is, the way it has been organised – and the techniques that the writer uses in order to organise it this way.

You could write about:
- the beginning and ending
- techniques that give you clues that something is going to happen
- techniques that stress certain ideas in the extract.

This question is worth 10 marks.

> **structure**: the way a text has been organised in order to create certain effects

Timing

You will already have read the extract. There are 10 marks for this question and you need to analyse language and structural points, so aim to spend about 12 minutes answering it.

What the examiner is looking for

The examiner is looking for evidence that you can:
- analyse how writers use language
- consider the effect of the structure of the text
- support what you say with relevant quotations
- use subject terminology well.

In this unit you will revise how to write about:
- language
- the effects of structure
- narrative perspective
- how ideas are developed.

> **Exam tip**
>
> Note that Question 4 is not the only question where you can write about structure. Apart from Question 1, you can look at structure in any of your answers in Section A, if you find an interesting point worth analysing. However, do not *just* focus on structure. Aim to spend most of your time analysing language.

Looking at structure

REVISED

Consider what the writer's aims might have been in opening each paragraph as they do. The opening might establish setting, begin with a dramatic event or give you details about character or setting. A certain mood might be created to hint that the text that follows will be a happy one, or a serious one. From the opening lines, the reader will start to make judgements about what might follow.

Tasks

Read the following openings from texts that have appeared in earlier units in this book. After each, consider what questions you may have about later events. By doing this, you will be thinking about how the writer has captured your interest.

For example:

> The gravel drive was short but still served to cut the house off from the rest of the street. I took a few tentative steps away from the warm glow of the streetlamps.

You could ask the following:

- What has happened in this house, or what will happen?
- Why is someone visiting it?

1 Now try these yourself:

a

> What we saw when we stood from our picnic was this: a huge grey balloon, the size of a house, the shape of a teardrop, had come down in the field. The pilot must have been halfway out of the passenger basket as it touched the ground. His leg had become entangled in a rope.

b

> 'Arthur!' – his voice a shriek – 'I'm going to fall.'
>
> 'Good,' Arthur said.
>
> The word that would haunt him for the rest of his life.

c

> The cop got off his motorcycle and leaned the machine sideways onto its prop stand. Then he took off his gloves and placed them carefully on the seat. He was in no hurry now. He had us where he wanted us and he knew it.

d

> What was Struan, apart from a sawmill? A sorry bunch of stores lined up along a dusty main street, with nothing in them anyone would want to buy.

2 Now develop this, by selecting particular words and phrases that have prompted you to ask these questions.

For example:

> The gravel drive was short but still served to cut the house off from the rest of the street. I took a few tentative steps away from the warm glow of the streetlamps.

a What has happened in this house, or what will happen?

b Why is someone visiting it?

Words and phrases that made me ask these questions were 'cut the house off', 'tentative steps' and 'away from the warm glow'.

3 Now select your own words and phrases from the four openings above. Note, when constructing an opening, the writer is not hoping that their reader will guess all the events that will follow in the text, but rather to capture the reader's interest in the story.

Tasks

Re-read the following extract:

> The gravel drive was short but still served to cut the house off from the rest of the street. I took a few tentative steps away from the warm glow of the streetlamps, until I was inside the gate and technically, now on private land.

> **Exam tip**
>
> When writing about structure, avoid phrases such as 'This makes you think', 'This makes you read on'. They are too general to mean much by themselves. Instead, explain what the passage has made you think about, or why the text interests you enough to read on and use evidence from the text to support what you say.

The following student has put their ideas together from the exercises in the unit and written a response to the question:

How does the writer make these lines tense for the reader?

1 Use the grade descriptors that follow to decide what grade you would award this answer.

embedded quotation shows confidence with language

engages with the question

thoughtful explanation precise evidence shows attention to language

shows awareness of structure

comments on structure

embedded quotation

> The writer makes these lines tense for the reader by explaining that the gravel drive 'cut the house off' from the street. This makes it sound distant from civilisation and suggests to the reader that something bad might happen in this lonely place. The narrator says that they took 'tentative steps'. The adjective used here conveys fear because the narrator clearly doesn't really want to go towards this house. Again, this indicates to the reader that there is something negative about this place. This seems to foreshadow danger and maintains our interest. Once the narrator steps 'away from the warm glow' of the streetlamps, you can imagine the darkness around them. This increases tension and you receive a sense of foreboding about this place.

2 It would also be useful to re-read the student's response and find where they make a point about language and where they make a point about structure. This is what the examiner will be looking for. For example:
  ○ language point: 'tentative steps' suggest fear
  ○ structure point: something bad might happen in this lonely place.
Try to find two more examples of each from the student's answer.
Answers:
  ○ language points: 'cut the house off' suggests it's distant from civilisation; 'away from the warm glow' suggests darkness
  ○ structure points: 'tentative steps' seems to foreshadow danger; 'away from the warm glow' conveys a sense of foreboding.
Grade awarded: 7

foreboding: a feeling that something bad will happen

foreshadowing: a warning or indication of a future event

Assessment comment

Notice that this student has not used the phrases, 'This makes you think', or, 'This makes you read on'. Instead, they have chosen precise references and commented on these, saying that the clues 'foreshadow danger' and they feel 'a sense of foreboding' when reading this passage.

Mark scheme

Grades	Descriptors
9	Insightful analysis of how the writer uses language and structure to create tension. Purposeful evidence supports points.
7, 8	Perceptive analysis of how the writer uses language and structure to create tension. Uses precise evidence to support points.
5, 6	Thoughtful analysis of how the writer uses language and structure to create tension. Uses well-chosen evidence.
4	Some understanding of how tension is created and awareness of the organisation of events. Uses relevant evidence and starts to look at language choices.
3	Awareness of tension. Straightforward textual references. May comment on the writer's choice of words.
1, 2	Emerging awareness of the frightening parts of the text, with simple comments made. May find some basic evidence.

Tasks

1 Read the following opening. Decide:
   a what you learn about the narrator
   b what you learn about the setting
   c what sort of a mood is created.

> The beginning is simple to mark. We were in sunlight under a turkey oak, partly protected from a strong, gusty wind. I was kneeling on the grass with a corkscrew in my hand, and Clarissa was passing me the bottle – a 1987 Daumas Gassac. This was the moment, this was the pinprick on the time map: I was stretching out my hand, and as the cool neck and the black foil touched my palm, we heard a man's shout.
>
> (*Enduring Love*, Ian McEwan, 1997)

2 Now consider what predictions you might have about what will follow in the text, or what you would like to find out. Select specific words and phrases that give you the impression that the rest of the extract might be about a serious event.
   Answers: The narrator seems romantic and thoughtful in, 'This was the moment, this was the pinprick on the time map'. It's a pleasant setting, under a tree and protected from the wind. The mood is initially calm, then dramatic when a man shouts.

Developing ideas

Tasks

1 Reflect on the predictions you just made and the words and phrases you selected that gave you clues that a serious event might follow. For example, you might have chosen the following:
   ○ 'The beginning' – suggests that a dramatic event will follow.
   ○ 'protected from a strong, gusty wind' – makes you wonder if the wind will cause a problem later once they leave the shelter of the tree.
   ○ 'I was kneeling in the grass with a corkscrew in my hand' – sounds like they're having a picnic which creates a happy atmosphere, but you get a sense that this relaxed mood won't last.
   ○ 'a 1987 Daumas Gassac' – probably the name of an expensive wine. The narrator might have bought it for a special occasion.
   ○ 'This was the moment, this was the pinprick on the time map' – this sounds like a very memorable day.
   ○ 'I was stretching out my hand' – he seems to remember the details of that moment, as if something will happen to make it a day to remember.
   ○ 'we heard a man's shout' – suggests an accident or problem.

2 The following extract continues from where the last one left off, and tells you what happens next. Consider whether it answers any of the questions you had from reading the opening of the story.

> We turned to look across the field and saw the danger. Next thing, I was running toward it. The transformation was absolute: I don't recall dropping the corkscrew, or getting to my feet, or making a decision, or hearing the caution Clarissa called after me. What idiocy, to be racing into this story and its labyrinths, sprinting away from our happiness among the fresh spring grasses by the oak. There was the shout again, and a child's cry, enfeebled by the wind that roared in the tall trees along the hedgerows. I ran faster. And there, suddenly, from different points around the field, four other men were converging on the scene, running like me.
>
> (*Enduring Love*, Ian McEwan, 1997)

3 Read over the list below of ideas you might have considered when you first read the opening to the story. Do you now learn anything more about:

  a dramatic events?

  b the effect of the wind?

  c the spoiling of the happy atmosphere?

  d foreshadowing (clues that suggest these events will affect his future life)?

  e ideas that suggest an accident or problem?

4 Considering both the opening and the second extract from this story, now write your answer to the question:

How is this opening structured to engage the reader?

Use the previous mark scheme to help you grade your answer.

> **Exam tip**
>
> Don't just write about what happens in the given extract. You will be awarded marks for analysing language and structure, not re-telling the story.

Narrative perspective

REVISED

You might have noticed that both the earlier extract about the creepy house and the previous one about an unfolding accident are written in first person narrative. Read back over the extracts and start to consider the effects of choosing this narrative perspective.

Tasks

1 Make a list of the pros and cons of both narrative approaches. You will be able to use this information in your exam when commenting on the narrative approach of the given extract. Aim to list one more advantage and disadvantage for each narrative approach.

First person narrative		Third person narrative	
Advantages	**Disadvantages**	**Advantages**	**Disadvantages**
There is an intimacy between the narrator and reader.	The narrator doesn't usually comment much on themselves.	The narrator is unlikely to be as biased as a first person narrator.	It might take the reader longer to 'warm' to the characters.

You could have added:

  ○ **first person narrative advantages**: the narrator's feelings are clear

  ○ **disadvantages**: there is usually just one focus on a character or event at a time

  ○ **third person narrative advantages**: the narrator can 'go anywhere' in the story, focusing on any character, time or place

  ○ **disadvantages**: a character's feelings may not be as clear as the narrative approach is not personal.

2 Read the following extracts. Identify the **narrative perspective** of each. Select a phrase that you used to identify this. Comment on how the narrative perspective engages your interest. For example:

Hannah sits on the bench, the phone in her hand. She wills it to ring but it stays stubbornly silent. She turns it off and back on again, then lifts it aloft to better pick up signal. Nothing. She sighs and stuffs it back into her bag.

'Third person narrative is employed, shown in the use of a name, and the phrase "She sighs". The writer seems to be observing Hannah, and conveys her feelings of desperation and annoyance to encourage the reader to wonder who she is waiting for a call from.'

> **first person narrative**: the story is narrated by a character who is speaking about him or herself or giving an account of events that they were involved in
>
> **third person narrative**: the story is told by a narrator who isn't involved in the story themselves; they can focus on any character or place in the story and use 'he', 'she' or the characters' names to tell their story
>
> **narrative perspective**: this is the form used to tell the story; look to see if your exam text is written in first person narrative or third person narrative

3 Now try these yourself.

Text A

'Hmmm …' the elder officer says, 'are you in work tomorrow?'

'Yes,' I falter. This is worrying. The last thing I want is for the police to turn up at work. I quickly cover my nervous answer. I don't want them to think I have anything to hide. 'I arrive at work at about 8.30 in the morning, if you need me.'

'Don't worry, Miss Lycett. I'm sure we can get all the information we need from you today. It's just useful for our officers to know where you'll be if we need you.'

I nod and try to look thoughtful. My insides are churning.

Text B

The play was some sort of detective story; what Jo's mother would have called a 'whodunnit'. Once she thought of her mother, the old guilt came rushing back, and, all at once, thoughts of those tiresome conversations they used to have in front of the television. Her mother would chat through any programme, then ask endless questions about what was going on. 'Why don't you just *listen* to it?' Jo would snap, then her mother would fall silent and look sad. Jo knew that she wouldn't be having those conversations any more and she had the rest of her life to regret it.

Answers:

Text A: first person narrative. The speaker is clearly worried. Her feelings are made clear to us.

Text B: third person narrative. The writer focuses on Jo as a privileged viewpoint for the reader.

> **Exam tip**
>
> Although precise, single-word quotation is usually a high-grade skill, you will need a *phrase* to support points you make about narrative perspective. Do not say, 'I can tell it's first person because it says "I".' This comment is too simple to earn marks. Aim for a slightly longer quote and a more thoughtful comment.
>
> For example: 'The first person narrative approach is clear in "My insides are churning" and indicates that the character is worried about something.'

Use of tense

REVISED ☐

The writer's choice of tense can affect the reader's reaction to a story:

- Use of present tense creates a sense of immediacy. It's as if the story is happening now and anything could unfold. The reader is going through the story at the same time as the characters, as if both are experiencing events together. The benefit of this approach is a sense of closeness to characters, but the disadvantage is that tension devices, such as foreshadowing, can't be used as the characters don't know what will unfold.

- Use of the past tense is a more usual choice for a writer. It allows more range in story-telling, as the writer can move between any point in the character's story, reflect on events and hint at what will come later.

Tasks

Identify whether these extracts are written in the present or the past tense. Comment on the characters' feelings in each. How has each writer used tense choice to make their character's feelings clearer?

For example:

Sylvie strokes the dog and looks at me with mournful eyes. I can't bring myself to tell her, so I just stare at the ground.

'The narrator obviously has bad news to tell the other character, and doesn't want to upset her by saying it. The use of present tense involves the reader in this moment.'

1 Now you try.

a

It was one of those biting, cold days where the wind whips right through you and all you can think about is how uncomfortable you are. I certainly felt uncomfortable, but I would have felt a lot worse if I'd known how the day was about to unfold.

b

The machine blips somewhere above my head. I try to wriggle round in the bed to see it, but Doctor Ford places a kindly but firm arm on my shoulder and frowns. I'm not sure whether that frown means that I shouldn't be moving or whether he's frowning at whatever that bleeping noise means. I don't know and I don't want to ask.

Answers:

a Past tense – discomfort – 'would have felt a lot worse' shows the writer is looking back and worse is to come, which clarifies feelings.

b Present tense – worried – there is a sense of immediacy as if we are in the moment too.

Structural techniques

In addition to foreshadowing later events, and using a particular narrative perspective or choice of tense, a writer may use other structural techniques in order to maintain the reader's interest and emphasise certain elements of the story.

Read the following examples of each technique and the comments on their effects. Remember that each technique will not have exactly the same effect in every text you read, but the examples below are a good starting point. Aim to learn these.

- **Repetition**: *'Maybe she would tell Lisa. Maybe she would tell Lisa and then walk out, or maybe she would be a coward and do neither.'* Repetition gives emphasis to a particular idea in the text.
- **Dialogue**: *'"I'm desperately sorry," I murmured, lowering my eyes. Looking down, she couldn't see my smirk or the insincerity in my eyes.'* Dialogue gives voice to characters, conveying their personality and making them more convincing. In the given example, the reader is also able to see the difference in what the character says and what they really think.
- **Contrasts**: *'He stepped from the glare of the sun to the darkened cool of the church.'* The striking difference conveyed by contrasts indicates a new focus or shift in the story.
- **Short paragraphs**: *'From his window, Carl saw her leave the house and rush to the waiting car. The man in the driver's seat leaned over and kissed her. "Got you," Carl thought. He reached for the gun.'* Short paragraphs focus on a particular event or thought, emphasising its importance in the story.
- **Long sentences**: *'She went out, locking the classroom door behind her and scanning the corridor for anyone who might have seen.'* Long sentences contain several clauses. They can convey detail and develop ideas.
- **Simple sentences**: *'He posted the letter.'* A simple sentence contains one clause, made up of a subject ('He') and a verb ('posted'). It conveys information simply and bluntly.
- **Part sentences**: *'Why not?'* A part sentence is incomplete as it does not contain a verb. It conveys an idea briefly and our understanding of it relies on the previous or following sentence.

subordinate clause: a subordinate clause is dependent on a main clause to make sense; for example, '**When the doorbell rang**, she opened the door' – the bold section is the subordinate clause as it does not make sense by itself

compound sentence: in a compound sentence, both clauses make sense independently and can be joined by a conjunction or semi-colon; for example, 'Lia threw a rock and **it smashed the window**'

complex sentence: a complex sentence contains a main clause and at least one subordinate clause; for example, 'Duncan hit the cyclist as he swerved into the left-hand lane'

conjunction: a joining word; for example, 'and', 'but', 'because'

Task

Read this extract from a story.

> The head juror stands. He looks steadfastly at the judge, who is gathering his papers, as if the verdict has already been delivered. It is 5 p.m. in Courtroom Number Four, and the minute hand on the court clock that has ticked out every second of this arduous case seems to pause. The jury look at their spokesman; they are one body who will decide the fate of Tom Watson.
>
> Tom is sinking towards his seat but he is too early. His fate is not sealed. Not yet.
>
> 'Can you remain standing please, Mr Watson?' the judge says.
>
> Tom's barrister nods at him slowly. It's meant to convey encouragement but it could affirm what his defence team has known all along. The head juror interprets the nod to mean that he should speak. The clock reads 5.01. A cloud passes over the sun outside and the window's afternoon brightness turns to a momentary darkness slanting across Tom's face.
>
> It is unfortunate timing that a siren blares in the street outside just as the verdict is delivered. The spectators cannot hear it and neither can the judge, who cranes forward in his seat.
>
> Tom hears it.
>
> He hears it as his hands slip from their grip on the rail, and his vision blurs
>
> This time, the judge does not ask him to remain standing.

1 Identify:

- ○ foreshadowing
- ○ contrasts
- ○ third person narrative
- ○ short paragraphs
- ○ present tense
- ○ long sentences
- ○ repetition
- ○ simple sentences
- ○ dialogue.

You may have selected the following:

- ○ foreshadowing – 'A cloud passes over the sun', 'momentary darkness'.
- ○ third person narrative, present tense, short paragraph and simple sentence – 'Tom hears it.'
- ○ repetition – 'Tom hears it. He hears it …'
- ○ dialogue – 'Can you remain standing please …'
- ○ contrasts – 'brightness turns to a momentary darkness'
- ○ long sentence – third sentence.

2 Now, use all the techniques that you have found to help you answer the question:

How does the writer make this part of the story tense?

Mark scheme

Read over your answer and try to decide what grade you would award your response.

Grades	Descriptors
9	Analyses the subtleties of the techniques used. A wide range of structural techniques are analysed with purposeful evidence to support points.
7, 8	Perceptive analysis of how the writer uses language to create tension. A good range of structural techniques are analysed with precise evidence to support points.
5, 6	Thoughtful analysis of how the writer uses language to create tension. A range of structural techniques are analysed with use of well-selected evidence.
4	Some understanding of how language and organisation create tension. Uses relevant evidence.
3	Awareness of tension. Straightforward textual references.
1, 2	Emerging awareness of the tension in the text, with simple comments made.

Looking at endings

Of course, the ending of your extract is unlikely to be the very end of the novel from which the passage has been taken. Despite this, the writer will still be aware of the structure of their text and there may be a sense of finality in the extract's close, or **tension devices** that hint at events beyond your extract that will unfold later in the novel.

> **tension device**: a technique used to create suspense in a text

Tasks

1 Look back in this unit and re-read the two extracts about the unfolding accident, taken from *Enduring Love* by Ian McEwan. They were both taken from Chapter 1 of the novel. Below is the ending of Chapter 1. A man is trying to stop a hot air balloon from drifting away but he is holding on to its rope by himself and the wind has taken him and the balloon up into the air. Read the ending and consider which events are exciting.

> He was two hundred yards away now, and perhaps three hundred feet above the ground. Our silence was a kind of acceptance, a death warrant. Or it was horrified shame, because the wind had dropped, and barely stirred against our backs. He had been on the rope so long that I began to think he might stay there until the balloon drifted down or the boy came to his senses and found the valve that released the gas, or until some beam, or god, or some other impossible cartoon thing, came and gathered him up. Even as I had that hope, we saw him slip down right to the end of the rope. And still he hung there. For two seconds, three, four. And then he let go. Even then, there was a fraction of time when he barely fell, and I still thought there was a chance that a freak physical law, a furious thermal, some phenomenon no more astonishing than the one we were witnessing, would intervene and bear him up. We watched him drop. You could see the acceleration. No forgiveness, no special dispensation for flesh, or bravery, or kindness. Only ruthless gravity. And from somewhere, perhaps from him, perhaps from some indifferent crow, a thin squawk cut through the stilled air. He fell as he had hung, a stiff little black stick. I've never seen such a terrible thing as that falling man.

2 Once you have decided which events are exciting, re-read the extract and consider *how* the writer makes these events exciting. Remember to reflect on the techniques that have been covered earlier in this unit.

You may want to write about:

○ the foreshadowing in 'a death warrant'

○ the effect of first person narrative

○ the use of the past tense

○ the contrast of the silence and stillness against the man's 'thin squawk'

○ long, complex sentences

○ part sentences in 'For two seconds, three, four' and 'Only ruthless gravity.'

Test yourself

The following extract is taken from the opening of a novel about a man who is arrested for a crime he knows nothing about.

Answer the question:

How does the writer make these lines tense for a reader?   (10 marks)

Consider both language and structure when writing your answer. You must refer to the text to support your points, using relevant subject terminology where appropriate.

> Someone must have been telling lies about Josef K, he knew he had done nothing wrong but, one morning, he was arrested. Every day at eight in the morning he was brought his breakfast by Mrs Grubach's cook – Mrs Grubach was his landlady – but today she didn't come. That had never happened before. K waited a little while, looked from his pillow at the old woman who lived opposite and who was watching him with an inquisitiveness quite unusual for her, and finally, both hungry and disconcerted, rang the bell. There was immediately a knock at the door and a man entered. He had never seen the man in this house before. He was slim but firmly built, his clothes were black and close-fitting, with many folds and pockets, buckles and buttons and a belt, all of which gave the impression of being very practical but without making it very clear what they were actually for.
>
> 'Who are you?' asked K, sitting half upright in his bed.
>
> The man, however, ignored the question.

(*The Trial*, Franz Kafka, 1925)

Answers on p. 99

How to prepare for the exam

Re-read any of the extracts used earlier in this book and see what structural techniques you can find in them. Consider their effect.

Component 1, QA5 Evaluating critically

What this question involves

For Question 5, you are likely to be asked to **evaluate** a text critically and support this with references from the text.

Evaluating a text means to give your views and opinions on it, and say what you think and feel about characters, relationships or events. You may have to consider quite a large section of the extract or, sometimes, the whole extract. Evaluating 'critically' means that you will assess what you read. It does not necessarily mean that you *criticise* it.

You might be asked to:
● consider a statement about a text and decide how far you agree with it
● evaluate a character's behaviour or give your opinion on events.

This question is worth 10 marks.

Timing

You will already have read the extract but you will need to re-read the specified lines or, in some cases, the whole extract again. There are 10 marks for this question. Aim to spend about 12 minutes answering it.

What the examiner is looking for

The examiner is looking for evidence that you can:
● understand what it means to evaluate critically
● respond to the given question by evaluating an aspect of the text
● support what you say with appropriate textual references.

In this unit you will revise how to:
● give your opinion on something
● decide how far you agree with a given statement
● find evidence from the text to support your opinion
● explain how evidence supports your view.

Questions that ask you to evaluate   REVISED

Task

Read the following text. In this extract, a newspaper editor, Vernon Halliday, is in his office before an important meeting.

> For the first time in the day, Vernon found himself alone. His plan was simple. He quietly closed the door to the outer office, kicked off his shoes, switched off his phone, swept the papers and books from his desk – and lay on it. There were still five minutes before morning conference and there was no harm in catching a quick snooze. He had done it before – and it must be in the paper's interests to have him on top form. As he settled he had an image of himself as a massive statue dominating the lobby of Judge House, a great reclining figure hewn from granite: Vernon Halliday, man of action, editor. At rest. But only temporarily, because conference was due to start and already – dammit – people were wandering in. He should have told Jean to keep them out. He loved the stories told in pubs at lunchtimes of the editors

of old; the great V.T. Halliday, you know, of Pategate fame, who used to conduct his morning conferences lying on his desk. They had to pretend not to notice. No one dared say a thing. Shoeless. These days they're all bland little men, jumped-up accountants.

(*Amsterdam*, Ian McEwan, 1998)

The question given in the exam was:

Evaluate the way Vernon is presented in this passage.   (10 marks)

To answer this, prepare by responding to the following questions:
● What is the text about?
● What can you **infer** (work out) about Vernon?
● What are your thoughts and feelings about him?
● What is your opinion about the language used?
● What do you think about the techniques the writer uses?

> **inference**: a conclusion made based on information, evidence and reasoning

A student has begun to answer the exam question by working their way through the first two bullet points. Read their answer so far.

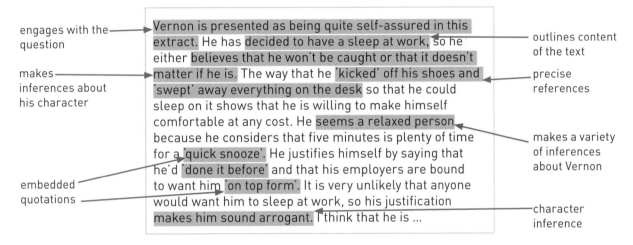

engages with the question

makes inferences about his character

embedded quotations

outlines content of the text

precise references

makes a variety of inferences about Vernon

character inference

Vernon is presented as being quite self-assured in this extract. He has decided to have a sleep at work, so he either believes that he won't be caught or that it doesn't matter if he is. The way that he 'kicked' off his shoes and 'swept' away everything on the desk so that he could sleep on it shows that he is willing to make himself comfortable at any cost. He seems a relaxed person because he considers that five minutes is plenty of time for a 'quick snooze'. He justifies himself by saying that he'd 'done it before' and that his employers are bound to want him 'on top form'. It is very unlikely that anyone would want him to sleep at work, so his justification makes him sound arrogant. I think that he is …

1 Now continue this answer by responding to the final three bullet points, to answer the question:
Evaluate the way Vernon is presented in this passage.   (10 marks)
You must refer closely to the text to support your answer.
Suggested answers:
○ He seems a busy man as he's alone, 'for the first time in the day'.
○ He's forward-thinking as he's planned this – 'His plan was simple.'
○ He's willing to take risks.
○ He behaves oddly, considering that he's at work.
○ He seems presumptuous in assuming his employers wouldn't mind.
○ He's vain – imagines himself as a statue for others to admire – 'massive', 'dominating' and 'great' show his sense of self-importance.
○ He defines himself as a 'man of action'. (Ironic as he's having a rest!)
○ He's short-tempered and curses – 'dammit' – when he's disturbed.
○ He sounds controlling – 'He should have told Jean to keep them out.'
○ He believes he should be able to do what he likes and admires those who do.
○ He's critical and judgemental – 'These days they're all bland little men'.

> **Exam tip**
>
> When you are asked to evaluate, it can be useful to consider a structure of:
> ● looking at overall content – seeing what you can infer about the character, place or event you are asked to evaluate
> ● analysing language – analysing technique.

Questions that ask you to respond to a statement

Another way that you may be asked to evaluate the text is by responding to a statement about it, then explaining how far you agree or disagree with that statement.

A writer may present a character or event in a certain way so that you feel sympathetic or you may be encouraged to feel dislike. In this way, the writer is influencing your reaction so that you feel a particular way. You will need to recognise and analyse what language and techniques have been used in order to make you feel like this.

> **Exam tip**
>
> When you are asked how far you agree with a statement, you should look for points that support the statement and points that contradict it. You can then draw an overall conclusion about the statement based on an evaluation of the points you have found.

Tasks

Read the following extract.

> Finding a role for a man of Hector's 'talents' had been difficult. For a time, the conventional wisdom was that the public would be best served by keeping Hector hidden in the bowels of the building, 'helping' with records. But the increase in computerisation had put an end to that. Though specifically forbidden to touch anything that had switches, buttons, lights or made a humming noise, Hector's mere presence seemed somehow perilous to the proper function of electronic equipment. 'He's a human virus,' declared the sergeant in charge. 'Get him out of here.' A spell on the desk in the station had brought complaints from the public that they had got better service from Mid-Yorks Water. Finally, when the local paper supported a campaign to get bobbies back on the beat, the Assistant Chief Constable said, 'Well, we can manage *that*,' and Hector was returned into the community.
>
> But not without some necessary precautions. He had to radio in every thirty minutes, or a car was sent out to look for him. If his assistance was required in any matter more serious than a request for the time, he had to contact the station for instructions. And in particular, he was strictly forbidden to make any attempts to direct traffic, as his last venture in that area had resulted in a gridlock which made the Chief Constable miss a train.
>
> (*On Beulah Height*, Reginald Hill, 1998)

The question given in the exam was:

'In this extract, the writer presents Constable Hector as a useless policeman.' To what extent do you agree with this view?   (10 marks)

You should write about:
a your own impressions of Hector
b how the writer has created these impressions.

You must refer closely to the text to support your answer.

1 Now prepare for this question by considering the following:
    a What is the writer's opinion of Hector? What evidence can you find to support this?
    b What is the writer's opinion of Hector's employers – that is, the sergeant and the Assistant Chief Constable? What evidence can you find to support this?
    c What are your own thoughts and feelings about Hector?
2 You may wish to build a case for Hector being presented as useless and a case against this, using the approaches taken so far in this unit. Use the following table to help you. These arguments need not be equal. Some ideas have already been completed for you.

	Negative view of Hector	Positive view of Hector
Content	The extract is about an inefficient policeman causing chaos wherever he goes.	
Inferences about Hector and his employers		Hector seems useless, but his intentions are good. He tries to do his job. His employers try to find tasks that suit his limited abilities.
Language that gives you these impressions of the characters		Hector thinks he is 'helping'. He also makes 'attempts' to do his job.
Techniques that help to give you these impressions	Metaphor, 'He's a human virus'.	Inverted commas around 'helping' suggest Hector and his employers have very different views about his abilities.

Suggested answers:

○ Inferences: he can't do his job properly. His employers try to keep him out of the way.

○ Language: 'talents' is used mockingly; 'hidden', 'returned into the community' and 'forbidden' show how his employers try to control him.

○ Techniques: sentences starting with 'But' go on to show the negative effects of Hector's work.

3 Now write up your points from the table above into a paragraph, to respond to the statement:

'In this extract, the writer presents Constable Hector as a useless policeman.'

End with a sentence summarising whether you agree with the statement, disagree, or partly agree.

4 Now mark your answer, awarding it a grade from the grade descriptor table below.

Mark scheme

Grades	Descriptors
9	Evaluates the presentation of Hector with subtle insight and detail. Well-selected and purposeful examples explain views. Perceptive analysis of the effect of language and techniques.
7, 8	Evaluates the presentation of Hector clearly and in detail. Chooses precise examples to explain views. Analyses the effect of language and the writer's techniques.
5, 6	Evaluates the presentation of Hector with understanding. Chooses convincing examples to support views. Explains clearly the writer's language choices and techniques.
4	Expresses an opinion of the character of Hector. Supports with relevant references. Some comments on the writer's techniques and language use.
3	Gives a personal opinion of the character of Hector. Supports with straightforward references. May make simple comments on the writer's choice of words.
1, 2	Expresses a simple, personal opinion. Uses basic textual references.

Test yourself

Read the passage and answer the question that follows.

Thirteen-year-old Rob has just begun 'going out' with his first girlfriend, Alison. In this extract, Rob sees Alison with another boy.

On the fourth night of our relationship I turned up in the park and Alison was sitting on the bench with her arm around Kevin Bannister. Nobody – not Alison, or Kevin, or me, said anything at all. I stung, and I blushed, and I suddenly forgot how to walk without being aware of every single part of my body. What to do? Where to go? I didn't want to fight; I didn't want to sit there with the two packets that marked out the path between the girls and the boys, and not looking up or behind me or to either side, I headed back towards the massed ranks of the single males hanging off the swingboat. Halfway, I made my only error of judgement: I stopped and looked at my watch, although for the life of me I don't know what I was attempting to convey, or who I was trying to kid. What sort of time, after all, could make a thirteen-year-old boy spin away from a girl and towards a playground, palms sweating, heart racing, trying desperately not to cry? Certainly not four o'clock on a late September afternoon.

(*High Fidelity*, Nick Hornby, 1995)

Evaluate the way Rob is presented in this passage.   (10 marks)

You should write about:
● your own thoughts and feelings about how Rob is presented
● how the writer has created these thoughts and feelings.

You should refer to the text to support your answer.

Answers on p. 99

How to prepare for the exam

Turn back in this book and choose an extract to re-read. As you read it, consider the structured approach of content, inferences, language, techniques and consider what you could say about each aspect.

Component 1, Section B
Creative prose writing

What this question involves

This question is worth 40 marks, with 24 marks being awarded for the content and organisation of your story and 16 marks for vocabulary, sentence structure, spelling and punctuation.

You should aim to write about 450–600 words.

Timing

You will have 45 minutes to write your story, with 10 minutes spent on planning and 35 minutes writing.

What the examiner is looking for

The examiner is looking for evidence that you can:
- use language creatively and imaginatively
- organise your story clearly
- use grammar, punctuation and spelling carefully.

In this unit you will revise how to:
- organise your story
- create character
- choose your vocabulary carefully
- use a range of techniques in order to create impact in your writing (such as the senses and onomatopoeia)
- improve your grammar, punctuation and spelling.

Some students say that they 'can't write stories'. Certainly, some people are better at it than others and those who read widely will know more about how characters and plot are created. However, you can certainly practise to become better at writing stories. The activities in this unit will show you how to do this.

Choosing your story

REVISED

You will have four options to choose from. Some of these will have a title, such as 'The Cheat' or 'Lost in the Snow'. Others will give you a scenario, such as 'Write about a time when you were nervous'. Another option may be a story opening, such as, 'Write a story which begins, "The small advertisement in the newspaper caught my eye."'

Task

1 Read the four options below and choose which you think you could write the best story on. You should make a choice within about four minutes.
   Choose **one** of the following titles for your writing:
   ○ **Either** (a) 'A Chance at Fame'.
   ○ **Or** (b) 'The Interview'.
   ○ **Or** (c) Write about a time when you broke something valuable.
   ○ **Or** (d) Write a story which begins: 'The teacher was looking straight at me and he was clearly furious.'

> **Exam tip**
>
> Whichever option you choose, make sure that you write whether you chose Option (a), (b), (c) or (d) in the margin of your answer booklet. If you don't do this, it can be difficult for your examiner to work out which one you have answered.

Do not pre-prepare an entire story before the exam. Better ideas are to:
- prepare descriptions of characters and settings that you can use in different stories
- have a 'stock' of good vocabulary to employ on the day
- think of times when certain events happened in your own life, as these provide good ideas that can be adapted in the exam.

Using your planning time

The examiner will be looking for evidence that you have organised your story well. This is why it is very important to use the ten minutes' planning time carefully. You should then have a clear idea of how your story will begin, develop and end.

An effective plan is:
1 a gripping opening (known as exposition)
2 the development of events (rising action)
3 the climax of events about two-thirds of the way through
4 the result of the climactic event (falling action)
5 a clear ending which ties up all the story threads.

Tasks

1 Using the given plan, jot down ideas for each bullet point for the titles below.

For example: 'The School Trip':

   a Gripping opening – trip to the Tower of London. Describe my feelings.

   b Development of events – argument with friend. I storm off. Miss tour of Tower.

   c Main event – hear friends coming. Hide in dungeon. Door sticks.

   d Result of the main event – friends hear call for help. Reconciled.

   e Ending – humiliation as class hears what happened but glad friends again.

2 Remember that the plan is for the content of your whole story and each point on the plan could be several paragraphs. Now try planning one of these:

   a 'The Audition'.

   b 'My Last Chance'.

   c Write about a time when you let a friend down.

   d Write a story that begins: 'I held the diary in my hands and wondered if I dared to read it.'

> **Typical mistakes**
>
> If you read a lot of books of a certain type, such as science-fiction or detective, you can probably write well in these genres. Otherwise, avoid **genres** you are unfamiliar with and write a story about events you are familiar with, such as those in your own life.

> **genre**: a type or style that includes particular characteristics, such as science-fiction, horror, romance or spy

Organising your work

Openings

You may wish to use a dramatic opening that begins the story at the height of the action. This type of exciting beginning should be fairly brief – one or two sentences – then you 'restart' the story in the second paragraph, building back up to the exciting event about two-thirds of the way through the story.

Tasks

1 Contrast the following two openings. Decide why the first is uninteresting and why the second is much better. They are both a response to the story title: 'The Dare':

> I woke up and got out of bed. I put on my dressing-gown and went downstairs for breakfast. I poured myself some cereal. It was Halloween and I was going to my friend's house because we were going to do a dare.

> Footsteps echoed on the upstairs corridor. I stifled a cry and bit the back of my hand to stop myself from sobbing as the echoing tread drew ever closer.
>
> Just three short hours before, I had been sitting safely at home …

> **Exam tip**
>
> Useful phrases to begin your second paragraph are: 'Just a short while before …', 'It all began when …', 'The day began calmly enough …', 'That morning, I had no idea that …', 'When I look back on it now …'.

2 Read the following story titles and write a first paragraph of just two sentences, which puts the reader straight into the action. Then write the opening phrase of your second paragraph, briefly setting up the events to this situation.
   a 'The Lie'.
   b Write about a time when something turned out better than expected.
   c 'A Surprising Gift'.

Developing your story

Your story's events should be linked. Show what caused the main action to happen and what the effect was. If you have planned carefully, your story will have this sense of unity.

Check the following:
- Have you made it clear who the characters are?
- Have you explained why a situation has occurred?
- Is there a clear sense of time?
- Does the ending link with the events that have happened?

It is difficult to appraise your own work. Ask someone else to read it or try writing a story and re-reading it a few days later.

> **Exam tip**
>
> If your story is well organised, events will follow logically. You should not use sub-headings in a story to 'sign-post' what is going on, such as 'Two hours later…'. Use instead: 'The next two hours passed in a blur…'

Task

1 Read the following extracts. Each includes a clumsy sub-heading that shows ideas have not been well organised. Replace each with a sentence that is part of the story.
   a The party was now in full swing and all I could hope was that Mum didn't come home early
   Three hours later.
   I saw the floodlights of Mum's car sweep across the drive and realised, to my horror, that she had returned.
   b I stood at the edge of the hockey pitch feeling bored. Suddenly, I heard my name being shouted and turned to see the ball catapulting towards my face.
   A few hours later.
   I opened my eyes and saw that I was in a hospital bed.

Endings

A story is a sequence of linked events. A story that has been structured carefully will have a satisfying ending. The reader should be left with a sense of completion. Even an open ending will link to the events that have preceded it and should not feel 'tagged on'.

Do not:
● end with waking from a dream
● fall into unconsciousness or die by using a phrase such as 'and then it all went black'
● finish with 'To be continued …'.

The most well-organised stories will link to how the story began or reflect on events. This strengthens their structure.

Task

1 Read these story endings. Decide which four are the most effective and why.
   a Alex closed his eyes and laid his head on Katie's shoulder. 'I'll never leave you again,' he whispered.
   b I heard my mum screaming my name and then I don't remember anything else.
   c She folded the letter, placed it in the hole and shovelled the dirt over it. The secrets that it held would remain there forever.
   d When I woke up from the coma it was many years later and I didn't remember anything that had happened.
   e Simone promised herself that she would never place her trust in a stranger again.
   Hopefully, you chose a, b, c and e as the most effective.

Creating character

REVISED

Your characters should be convincing. They need to sound like real people. Think of people that you know in order to help you write about your characters well.

Tasks

It is a good idea to prepare a range of character descriptions that you could use in any story. If you prepare a description for an older lady, for example, you could use this for the character of a grandparent, a teacher, a person at an audition or any number of other possibilities.

The prepared descriptions need only be brief. You need to consider:
● their appearance
● their personality
● the way they speak
● how they behave
● what others think of them.

For example, 'An old man':

Exam tip

Once you have about ten minutes left of the exam, you should be working on your ending. If you are nowhere near it, you will need to cut out some of the action. An accidental cliff-hanger ending shows that you were unable to control the story in the time available.

Assessment comment

Ending a has a clear resolution and links back to an event earlier in the plot. Ending c finishes the story conclusively and references an exciting event has happened and now needs to be kept a secret. Ending e comes to a decisive conclusion and shows what the character has learnt from events. By contrast, although Ending b is potentially quite exciting, the writer appears to die, so would not have been able to write the story. Ending d is unconvincing as years seem to have passed by.

- Appearance: wispy hair, lined skin, prominent veins, liver-spotted hands, home-knitted cardigan.
- Personality: obstinate and disagreeable.
- Way of speaking: loud, overbearing voice.
- How they behave: interrupts other people, poor manners.
- What others think: intimidated by him.

1 Now you try:
   a A middle-aged lady
   b A teenager
   c A young child
   d A baby

2 When we observe people, we often notice little things about them, such as a sticking-up fringe, bright buttons on a coat or the way that they walk. Now reflect on your ideas and try to add a small detail to each of your characters.

   For example, an old man: 'His fingernails were stubby and bitten and had a yellow tinge to them.'

   It is useful to learn a bank of ambitious words that you can use for your character descriptions. Try to learn and use some of the following synonyms.
   ○ Large: brawny, corpulent, portly, stout.
   ○ Thin: bony, emaciated, gaunt, haggard.
   ○ Old: elderly, mature, decrepit, withered.
   ○ Young: youthful, immature, infantile, juvenile.
   ○ Tall: statuesque, lofty, rangy, imposing.
   ○ Short: petite, diminutive, squat, slight.

   Also note that some have positive connotations ('petite') and some negative ('squat'). Make sure that you are confident with their meanings.

3 To write about your characters' feelings convincingly, aim to *show* how they are behaving, not just *tell* the reader. For example, instead of just telling the reader 'She felt tired in the car', you can show what this tired character might be doing to convey this. For example: 'Her shoulders slumped and her head edged closer to her folded arms.' Look at this picture of a woman. Write a few lines about how she might be feeling by describing her expression and body language.

4 Now put your ideas together. Choose one of the characters you have already planned. Write about four lines describing their appearance, personality, way of speaking and behaving and what others think about them. Include at least one small detail and convey something about the way they are feeling.

> **Typical mistakes**
>
> A common mistake in story-writing is to say that *everyone* was behaving in a certain way. For example: 'Everyone was screaming.' This is a lazy approach to writing. Instead, use the little details from your ideas to show the examiner that you are imaginative and creative.

Effective techniques

REVISED

Narrative perspective

As explained in the Component 1, Question 4 section of this book, the narrative perspective is the form used to tell the story. This can be first person narrative or third person narrative. In **first person narrative**, the story is narrated by a character who is speaking about him or herself. In **third person narrative**, the story is told by a narrator who isn't involved in the story themselves.

Tasks

Read the following extract that is written in third person narrative.

> Backing onto the football pitch, Mr Bellingham blew his whistle, waving to the stragglers. Half-heartedly, they started to run. Lorrimer brought up the rear, already out of breath, one hand pressed to a stitch in his side.
>
> 'Come on now, line up. Abbott and Kennedy, you pick the teams. Abbott, you start. And don't take all day about it. It's not the World Cup.' He turned away muttering, 'God help England if it was.'
>
> Kennedy's hand shot up. 'It's not fair, Sir. Abbott always picks first.'
>
> Mr Bellingham bared his teeth in a grin. 'Well, his name always begins with "A" doesn't it?'
>
> Abbott got in quickly. 'Harper.'
>
> 'Watson.'
>
> The names were called out, each name reducing the number of unselected boys until only Lorrimer was left.
>
> 'You see?' Kennedy complained, to nobody in particular. 'It's every week the same. Every week.'
>
> Abbott and his team were already jogging away up the field.

(*The Man Who Wasn't There*, Pat Barker, 1989)

1 Consider the following:
   a What are Kennedy's feelings?
   b What can you infer (work out) about Kennedy?
2 You will have noted that Kennedy feels this way of selecting teams is unfair. He seems fed up and outspoken.
   Now rewrite this extract as Kennedy, using first person narrative. Decide if your new version changes how the reader feels about him. For example, you might have included more on what he's thinking and made him a sympathetic character.

Using dialogue

The way characters speak will convey their personalities and attitudes.

Tasks

1 Re-read the dialogue in the previous extract. From the way that he speaks, how do you think Mr Bellingham feels about this lesson?
2 Continue this extract with a brief conversation between Kennedy and Lorrimer before the game begins. Their personalities and attitudes should be conveyed by what they say and how they say it.
3 Read the brief conversations below. By changing the verbs and adverbs, the characters' feelings are portrayed very differently. What differing impressions of the characters' moods do you receive?
   a 'You're late!' laughed Dad. 'Why didn't you come home an hour ago?'
   'My watch stopped,' I explained patiently.
   'Well, your cousins had to leave,' murmured Dad, turning away.
   b 'You're late!' screamed Dad. 'Why didn't you come home an hour ago?'
   'My watch stopped,' I snapped impatiently.
   'Well, your cousins had to leave,' retorted Dad, turning away.
4 Now you try. As in the previous example, keep the dialogue the same but change the verbs and adverbs used for the *way* the characters speak to create two conversations with different moods.
   'Where are you going?'
   'Home.'
   'Shall I come with you?'
   'There's no need.'

The senses

You will naturally rely quite a lot on the sense of sight in your story, as you describe what characters and settings look like, but you can make your story more creative if you also use the other senses.

Avoid a repetitive approach of 'I could see …', 'I could hear …', 'I could feel …', 'I could smell …', 'I could taste …'. Instead, vary your sentences.

For example: 'Her long, corn-coloured hair lifted in the cool breeze. The auburn leaves rustled as the wind strengthened, bringing the aroma of cut hay across the autumn afternoon.'

What senses did you find in this example?

Task

1 For each of the scenes below, jot down what you would see, hear, feel and smell in these places.
   a A shopping centre
   b A school canteen
   c A forest.

Onomatopoeia

You have just learnt how using the senses can bring a scene to life. Some students like to use **onomatopoeia** when including sounds in their stories. Be very careful with this as you can make your story sound unsophisticated. Non-standard capitalisation (when you write the sound in capital letters, for example 'CRASH!') is also to be avoided. It is a lazy way of trying to emphasise a loud sound when you can't really be bothered to describe it.

> **onomatopoeia**: a word for a sound that is similar to the noise the sound refers to; for example, 'bang', 'crash', 'screech'

Task

1 Compare the basic use of onomatopoeia below, with its improved description.
   'The book fell. BANG!'

   ↓

   'The book slipped from his hands. Before he could catch it, it hit the floor with a resounding thump.'
   Now you try. Improve each example:
   a The doorbell rang. DING DONG!
   b I dropped the glass. CRASH!
   c The bomb exploded. BOOM!

Improving vocabulary

REVISED

As you are being assessed on the way that you write, you should aim to use a range of ambitious vocabulary.

> **Typical mistakes**
>
> Although it is a good idea to use a thesaurus beforehand to 'stock up on' and learn some effective vocabulary, don't use words that are so unusual you have no idea what they mean. Use vocabulary which is ambitious but not obscure.

Task

1 As your story will have some action in and may also include dialogue, you are most likely to need a variety of words for 'said' and 'go'. Add to the list below. Aim to think of five more **synonyms** for 'said' and five that mean a movement forward. Make sure that you know what they all mean if you intend to use them in the exam.
  ● said: bellow, chorus, declare, interject …
  ● go: amble, caper, dawdle, saunter …

> **synonym**: a word that means the same or nearly the same as another word
>
> **antonym**: a word opposite in meaning

Tasks

Read the Grade 4 description below.

basic vocabulary ⟶ | The desert was big and there was sand everywhere. I could see some plants in the distance. | ⟵ uninspiring description
⟵ no detail

1 Now compare it to the Grade 9 description of the same place.

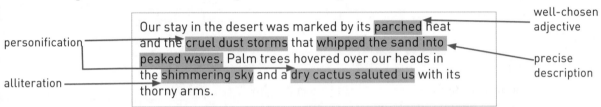

personification ⟶
alliteration ⟶

Our stay in the desert was marked by its parched heat and the cruel dust storms that whipped the sand into peaked waves. Palm trees hovered over our heads in the shimmering sky and a dry cactus saluted us with its thorny arms.

⟵ well-chosen adjective
⟵ precise description

2 Use some of the following vocabulary to write a brief description of each place. You can also include the senses, small details and your own ambitious language choices.
  a An ordinary house in a town.
    Vocabulary: modest, understated, quintessential (typical).
  b A forest.
    Vocabulary: tranquil, serene, verdant (green).
  c An old, abandoned cottage.
    Vocabulary: ramshackle, dilapidated, decrepit.

> **Exam tip**
>
> Marks are awarded for effective descriptive writing in the exam, but remember that your story is not just a descriptive exercise. Aim to keep your descriptions brief and focused.

Improving grammar

REVISED

Remember that 40 per cent of the marks in the story-writing section are awarded for careful use of grammar, punctuation and spelling, so don't rush your writing so much that you make careless mistakes.

To achieve a good grade, your control of tense and agreement must be secure. This means that you must write in the same tense throughout your story and not move between the present and past tenses.

The best advice is to stay in the past tense throughout.

Task

1 Read the following section of a student's story. Identify the six tense changes and alter them so that the story is all in the past tense.

> It was my first day of work experience so I arrived at the school early. A mob of children began to appear at the door of the nursery. I feel nervous immediately and wasn't sure that I could cope with whatever lay ahead. The teacher tells me to open the door. The door opens and a barrage of children seems to flood in. I gasp at the number in the class – there must be forty of them!

The corrections are:

> It was my first day of work experience so I arrived at the school early. A mob of children began to appear at the door of the nursery. I **felt** nervous immediately and wasn't sure that I could cope with whatever lay ahead. The teacher **told** me to open the door. The door **opened** and a barrage of children **seemed** to flood in. I **gasped** at the number in the class – there must **have been** forty of them!

> **Typical mistakes**
>
> Avoid starting sentences with conjunctions, such as 'and', 'but' and 'because'. Their correct grammatical function is to join sentences.

Task

A common grammar error is to miss out a main verb in a sentence.

In the following example, the first sentence is correct but the second does not have a main verb.
- The alarm went off. Blaring in everybody's ears.

To correct this, the second sentence either needs to be linked to the first:
- The alarm went off, blaring in everybody's ears.

Alternatively, a main verb must be added:
- The alarm went off. **It was** blaring in everybody's ears.

1 Correct the second sentence in each of the examples below. You may wish to add a main verb, or rephrase the two sentences so that they are grammatically correct.
- **a** We laughed for ages. Giggling at our friends' jokes.
- **b** The fire was raging. Burning everything in sight.
- **c** The neighbours played loud music. Every day the same. There are a number of ways to rephrase these sentences, but suggestions could be:
- **a** We laughed for ages, giggling at our friends' jokes.
- **b** The fire was raging and burning everything in sight.
- **c** The neighbours played loud music. Every day was the same.

> **Typical mistakes**
>
> Avoid using 'gotten' and 'off of'. For example: 'I had only just *gotten* out of bed when Mum called me', 'I picked my slippers *off of* the floor and went downstairs.' This is not a secure use of grammar.

Practising punctuation

REVISED

Most punctuation errors in stories occur when writing dialogue. Ensure that:
- speech marks are used when someone is speaking
- speech starts with a capital letter
- punctuation goes inside the speech marks
- speech ends with a comma, full stop, exclamation mark or question mark
- you close the speech marks after the last word the character speaks
- you use a new line for a new speaker.

Task

1 Correct the punctuation in the dialogue below.

He was driving the car too quickly that was for sure

'Slow down' I yelled but he didn't hear me

The car just went faster and faster and I knew that we would never manage to take the corner at this speed. However somehow we made it.

The corrections are as follows:

He was driving the car too quickly, that was for sure.

Slow down!' I yelled, but he didn't hear me.

The car just went faster and faster and I knew that we would never manage to take the corner at this speed. However, somehow, we made it.

Checking your spelling

REVISED

To attain a Grade 5 in your story, most of your spelling, including that of irregular words, needs to be correct. You will need to practise words that you know you often spell incorrectly.

Tasks

1 Look through your class work and make a list of words you have often written incorrectly in the past.
2 Check that you can spell the words from the following list. They are some of the most commonly misspelled words in English.

○ definitely
○ independent
○ unnecessary
○ whether
○ embarrassing
○ disappear

○ dilemma
○ disappoint
○ tomorrow
○ argument
○ separate
○ accommodation

○ business
○ the singular – woman – and the plural – women

Test yourself

TESTED

Using the advice in this unit, choose **one** of the following titles for your writing:
● **Either** (a) 'Making a Choice'.
● **Or** (b) 'The Party'.
● **Or** (c) Write about a time when you let someone down.
● **Or** (d) Write a story which begins: 'I looked and saw that the door of the cage was open.'

Use the mark scheme in the final section of this book to grade your story.

Answers on p. 100

How to prepare for the exam

Observe people and note down how you would describe them. Start to keep a notebook of ideas, covering people of different ages and genders. You can use these ideas for characters in your exam story.

What does Component 2, Section A involve?

What you have to do

Component 2, Section A has six questions about two texts on a similar subject, totalling about 900–1,200 words. One will be from the nineteenth century and one from the twenty-first century. They will be non-fiction texts, so they could include articles, extracts from biographies or autobiographies, diaries, letters or reports. There are 40 marks available.

You have about an hour to complete this section. Spend around 10 minutes reading the texts and the questions carefully, then 50 minutes answering. Although you will answer on one text, then another, it is a good idea to read both texts at the beginning of the exam. It may take you a little longer to read and understand the nineteenth-century extract than the twenty-first century text. Do not rush your reading. In addition to making sense of the texts, you will need to be aware of any similarities between them and the techniques that the writers use in order to engage your interest.

The questions will usually be as follows:

Q A1	3 marks	This question will be based on the first text and divided into small parts, such as a, b and c. You will have to find a detail in the text for each part.
Q A2	10 marks	This is a language and technique question on the first text. You are likely to be asked how the writer uses language and techniques for a particular purpose, such as to convey a point of view.
Q A3	3 marks	This question will be based on the second text and divided into small parts. You will need to find short details in the text for each.
Q A4	10 marks	This question will be on the second text. You are likely to be asked what you think and feel about a situation in the text, or how successful the writer is in conveying a point of view to you.
Q A5	4 marks	This question will ask you to consider both texts. It is a search and find question where you will find short details and evidence from both texts.
Q A5	10 marks	You are likely to be asked to consider both texts again and compare their ideas and attitudes and how they are presented to you.

For the lower-mark questions, such as A1 and A3, you need to find short details in order to answer. You do not have to use your own words, although you can if you wish.

For the other questions, you will need to use evidence from the text to support your answer and explain your ideas. It is very important that you make clear which text you are referring to.

As in Component 1, there are no marks for spelling, sentence construction or punctuation in this section, but you should still express yourself clearly.

What this question involves

This question will be based on the first text and divided into smaller parts, such as a, b and c, worth 1 mark each. You will have to find a detail in the text for each. You should not waste time writing a lengthy answer or analysing the writer's language choices and techniques.

Timing

You will already have read the texts. There are 3 marks for this question, so aim to spend about 3–4 minutes answering it.

What the examiner is looking for

The examiner is looking for evidence that you can:
- select the right details from the text
- write them down clearly.

You can put your ideas into your own words or quote briefly from the text.

In this unit you will revise:
- how to find and use relevant information from the text.

> **Exam tip**
>
> Before you begin answering, be very clear about which text you are expected to answer on first. As both texts will be on a similar subject, you could end up trying to find the answer in the wrong one if you are rushing.

Task

Read the following short extract and question.

> Cornwall has been voted the most popular UK holiday destination for the second year running. The holiday hotspot has consistency scored highly for its beautiful beaches, family-friendly restaurants and the range of accommodation available.

A1 (a) For how many years in a row has Cornwall been voted the most popular UK holiday destination?   (1 mark)

1 Now read the following answers. Each gives the correct figure, but which do you think would be the best way to answer in the exam? Remember that your answers need to be brief and focused.
   a Cornwall has been voted the most popular UK holiday destination for the second year running.
   b Two years.
   The answer is two years. It says, 'for the second year running' so it is two years.
   Answer **b** is the most focused.

Test yourself

Read the following extract and answer the questions that follow.

Tough case to crack: the mystery of Britain's falling crime rate

According to the official statistics, crime is falling across Britain. It has been falling steadily for almost 20 years, despite the occasional spike in the statistics for some forms of crime. Over the past 12 months, the sharpest fall – 19 per cent – has been recorded in Northampton.

It is not just the people of Northampton who are perplexed by crime trends. While most people in England and Wales believe lawlessness to be falling in their area, the majority believe it to be rising nationally.

(*Guardian*, 31 August 2014)

A1:
a For how long have crime rates been falling across Britain?
b Where has the sharpest fall been recorded?
c What do most people believe is happening to crime rates nationally?

Answers on p. 101

How to prepare for the exam

Read any extract in this book and make up three 1-mark questions on it. Make sure that your answers only require a brief, focused response on a piece of explicit information.

Component 2, QA2 Analysing language

What this question involves

This question is usually based on the first text and requires you to look at how the writer conveys a certain view or idea. You will need to consider language, tone and structure and look at the way attitudes and arguments are presented.

This question is worth 10 marks.

Timing

You will already have read the texts. There are 10 marks for this question, so aim to spend about 10–12 minutes answering it.

What the examiner is looking for

The examiner is looking for evidence that you can:
● interpret the writer's ideas
● explain the effect of language choices
● find evidence for what you say.

In this unit you will revise:
● how language choices influence the reader's view
● how structure affects the reader's view
● what tone means and how it can affect our perception of a text.

Emotive language

REVISED

In a non-fiction text, the writer may be trying to convey a certain argument or point of view to you. In order to do this, the writer has made careful language choices that will influence how you feel about the topic of the text.

Tasks

1 Read the following sentences. Identify the emotive language in each. Decide how the writer's choice of words makes you feel about childhood obesity. For example:

disbelief = conveys the writer's shock

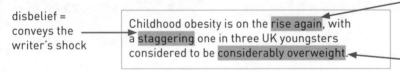
Childhood obesity is on the rise again, with a staggering one in three UK youngsters considered to be considerably overweight.

suggests that this is an existing problem that is becoming worse = the writer wants us to feel concern at the extent of it

shows the problem is extreme = the writer wants the reader to understand how far the problem has escalated

2 Now you try:
  a British graduates are now leaving university with remarkably bigger debts than their long-suffering American peers.
  b Schools are doing absolutely all they can to alert students to the hidden dangers of using social media recklessly.
  c Soaring sugar levels in supposedly healthy snacks are contributing to tooth decay.
  d Students at Warwick University have raised an impressive £7,500 to help the homeless and raise awareness of the horrors of sleeping rough.

3 In response to the example sentence about childhood obesity, two students have answered the question:

How does the writer show that childhood obesity is a problem?

You should comment on:

○ what he says

○ his use of language.

4 Look at the students' grades and the examiner's annotations of their answers.

Grade 4

Point – Evidence – Explanation structure is used ──→

It's a problem because it says 'Childhood obesity is on the rise again', which is getting worse. They say, 'with a staggering one in three UK youngsters considered to be considerably overweight', which sounds like a lot.

explanation is brief and it is not made clear *what* is 'getting worse'

'They' is incorrect as only one person has written this text

quote is quite long

no comment has been made about the writer's language choices

Assessment comment

This has the potential to be a good answer as it is well organised. However, points are general and little attention is paid to language.

Grade 7

shows understanding of how the writer wants us to react ──→

precise reference ──→

embedded quotation ──→

refers back to the question ──→

Childhood obesity is conveyed as a problem when the writer states that it is rising, 'again'. This suggests that the issue already existed but is now becoming worse. This is a worrying idea. The writer describes obesity levels as 'staggering', which conveys the extent of the problem as truly shocking. We are told that many young people are 'considerably' overweight. The adverb emphasises that the problem is extreme and is becoming out of control.

specific selection of evidence

question is kept firmly in mind throughout

subject terminology

Assessment comment

This is a well-organised, analytical answer. Language is looked at closely and the question is referred to throughout, showing clear control.

5 Now write up the notes you made on sentence **b** in question 2 above, to answer the following question:

How does the writer show that schools are trying to help students use social media responsibly?

You should comment on:

○ what he says

○ his use of language.

Exam tip

Avoid making general comments that don't focus on the specific words being used. Commenting that a word is 'good' or 'effective' is too general to be worth marks.

Fact and opinion

REVISED ☐

In order to impress a certain point of view on you, the writer might use **facts** and **opinions.** You need to be able to identify these so that you can judge whether the text is based on hard evidence or whether the writer is manipulating your feelings.

a **fact** is something that can be confirmed with proof; the most obvious facts are mathematical (2 x 2 = 4) or scientific (the human heart has four chambers)

an **opinion** involves belief; it is a point of view

Task

1 Identify whether the following statements are fact or opinion.

	Statement	Fact or opinion?
a	The word *karate* is Japanese for 'empty hand'.	
b	Every child knows that healthy eating is important.	
c	The Wright brothers built and flew the first aeroplane.	
d	Weekend television programmes are the best.	
e	Rugby is a better game than American football.	

Answers:

a fact   **b** opinion   **c** fact   **d** opinion   **e** opinion

Tasks

1 Read the following extract from an article about a skate park. Find three facts and three opinions from the extract.

> Stoke Plaza is the best skate park in the UK. Stoke-on-Trent city council spent an incredible half a million pounds creating this impressive venue in the Sneyd Green area of the city. With plenty of challenging banks, steps, ledges and handrails, the park does not disappoint visitors. If you skated its gnarly quarterpipes every day, you'd be a pro in no time.

Answers, three facts:

a It cost 'half a million pounds'.

b It's in Sneyd Green.

c It has 'banks, steps, ledges and handrails'.

Answers, three opinions:

a 'Stoke Plaza is the best skate park in the UK.'

b It 'does not disappoint'.

c If you skated it every day, 'you'd be a pro in no time'.

2 Copy and complete the table below to help you understand how the writer presents the skate park positively.

Technique used	Evidence from the text	Effect on the reader
Positive facts		
Engaging opinions		
Language that makes the park sound exciting		
Vocabulary that might appeal to teenagers		

Answers:

Technique used	Evidence from the text	Effect on the reader
Positive facts	'half a million pounds', 'plenty of challenging banks, steps, ledges and handrails'	Sounds expensive and well equipped = impressive
Engaging opinions	'the *best* skate park' (superlative), 'does not disappoint'	Sounds like it's worth a visit
Language that makes the park sound exciting	'incredible', 'impressive' 'challenging' (adjectives)	Fun, exhilarating
Vocabulary that might appeal to teenagers	'gnarly quarterpipes' , 'pro'	Informal language and slang appeals to the likely teenage audience

3 Now write up your notes on this extract to answer the following question:

How does the writer show that Stoke Plaza is an exciting place to skate? (10 marks)

You should comment on:

○ what he says

○ his use of language.

Mark scheme

Grades	Descriptors
9	Insightful analysis of the effects of language and technique. A wide range of vocabulary is analysed with purposeful evidence to support points. Exacting use of subject terminology.
7, 8	Perceptive analysis of the effect of language and technique. A good range of vocabulary is analysed with convincing evidence to support points. Precise use of subject terminology.
5, 6	Thoughtful analysis of how the writer uses language and techniques. A range of vocabulary is analysed with use of careful evidence. Subject terminology is used accurately.
4	Some understanding of how language and techniques are used. Relevant evidence to support points. Infrequent subject terminology.
3	Awareness of language choices and techniques. Straightforward evidence.
1, 2	Some copying of the text with simple comments made.

Structuring ideas

REVISED ☐

You will need to consider how the structure of the text affects the reader's view of it. This means that you need to look at the order of the information in the text and decide whether this order:

● makes the points clearer

● emphasises certain ideas

● affects the reader's response.

Tasks

Read the following extract.

The first hot balloon took to the skies in 1783. It was a short-lived experiment but one that encouraged the French Montgolfier brothers to try their own flight later that same year. This one was a success and hot air ballooning was born! The hobby involves a burner unit powering hot air into a huge balloon, with a suspended passenger basket below. Riders can soar and sail on the air to experience flight at its finest.

brief history of hot air ballooning to give background

summarises what the hobby involves early on in the text

Hot air ballooning used to be the preserve of the titled Victorian upper class. It was a way for rich gentlemen to pursue adventure. Although ballooning remains an expensive hobby for those who wish to own their own kit, it is a pursuit that everyone can experience by visiting a ballooning centre and trying a short, accompanied flight for themselves. Bristol's Ashton Court Estate takes keen balloonists across the Avon Gorge and the beautiful Somerset coastline, for reasonable rates.

explains how to get involved

examples

contrasts the old idea of ballooning as only for the rich with its accessibility now

Imagine floating with the birds across England's green and pleasant land and making memories that will last a lifetime. Book well in advance if you have a special event in mind, as flights tend to fill up early.

memorable idea leaves a lasting impression

advice at the end with the hope that the text has succeeded in interesting us in ballooning and we'd like to try it as a result

1 Consider the following question:

How does the writer make hot air ballooning sound appealing?

The annotations show you the effect of its structure. Consider:

○ why the writer begins as he does

○ how the writer develops the middle section

○ whether the ending leaves you with a particular impression.

2 Learn the following guide to the different effects of structure:

Beginnings: A non-fiction text will often start with one of the following:

○ outlining the topic

○ having a particular focus or scene

○ using a quote.

Middle: The middle section often maintains the reader's interest through:

○ examples

○ contrasting arguments

○ a shift in tone.

Endings: A non-fiction text will often end with one of the following:

○ a summary of the topic

○ a memorable idea

○ advice

○ a request for action.

3 Look again at the extract about hot air ballooning. Read the following example of the beginning of an answer to the question:

How does the writer make hot air ballooning sound appealing?

The student comments on structure, finds evidence and provides a thoughtful explanation. For example:

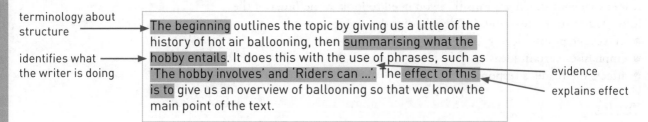

terminology about structure → The beginning outlines the topic by giving us a little of the history of hot air ballooning, then summarising what the hobby entails. It does this with the use of phrases, such as 'The hobby involves' and 'Riders can …'. The effect of this is to give us an overview of ballooning so that we know the main point of the text.

identifies what the writer is doing

evidence

explains effect

4 Re-read the extract about ballooning and continue the above answer. You may wish to use the following questions to guide you:

○ What effect does the **contrast** in the **middle** section have?

○ Why has the writer included an **example** of a location in the **middle** section?

○ Why is a pleasant balloon flight described towards the **end**?

○ Why finish with advice?

Answers:

○ The old idea of ballooning as only for the rich is contrasted with its relative accessibility now.

○ After 'hooking' us early on, the writer now includes an example of a ballooning location in case we are tempted to try it for ourselves.

○ The pleasant flight leaves a lasting impression on the reader.

○ The writer ends with advice, in the hope that the text has succeeded in interesting us in ballooning and we'd like to try it as a result.

Exam tip

When commenting on structure, you may find it useful to consider which are the *main* ideas of the text and which are the *supporting* ideas. The main idea is the point of the text, whereas the supporting ideas give less important information and details. The main ideas are usually introduced early on, and then developed with supporting points.

The tone of a text

The table below suggests useful vocabulary for describing a writer's **tone**. Ensure that you know the meaning of each word.

> **tone**: the mood implied by the text that expresses the writer's feelings or thoughts towards its topic

'The writer ...' (verbs that tell us *what* the writer is trying to do)	Positive	Negative	Neutral
	approves of celebrates commends defends	attacks mocks patronises ridicules scorns	conveys depicts describes illustrates portrays presents
Adverbs (-ly words that tell us *how* the writer is presenting their topic)	encouragingly jovially kindly positively proudly sensitively	aggressively angrily bitterly defensively pointedly sarcastically	carefully clearly flatly

> **Exam tip**
>
> Note that the writer's tone could be positive (supportive of the text's topic), negative (disapproving) or neutral (neither positive or negative, but simply giving you information). Be aware of the writer's possible bias. They may be using a positive or negative tone because they want to influence their reader to feel a particular way about a topic.

Tasks

The following text has been written in two different ways.
1 Use the words from the previous table to identify the tone of each.
2 What words helped you to identify the tone?
3 How do you think the writer wants us to feel towards the teenagers?

Text A

Most teenagers haven't a clue what they want to do for the rest of their lives. Pampered and protected by parents and teachers, they are nursed through their exams without the inclination to make big decisions. So, what can we do about Generation Snowflake? Rather than wrapping up these youths in cotton-wool, we should make them see the need to make rational decisions that reflect real life.

Text B

Most teenagers find it hard to decide what they want to do for the rest of their lives. Overwhelmed and stressed by workload, they are pushed through their exams without sufficient time for big decisions. So, what can we do about teen torment? Rather than push our youngsters, we can nurture and support them into making informed decisions that reflect their independence.

Answers, Text A:
1 Mocking and patronising.
2 'haven't a clue', 'Pampered and protected', 'nursed', 'without the inclination', 'Generation Snowflake', 'wrapping up these youths in cotton-wool', 'make them see the need', 'rational', 'real life'.
3 The writer wants us to feel that teenagers are overprotected and incompetent.

Answers, Text B:
1 Sympathetic and supportive.
2 'Hard', 'Overwhelmed and stressed', 'workload', 'pushed', 'without sufficient time', 'teen torment', 'push, nurture and support', 'informed', 'independence'.
3 The writer wants us to feel that teenagers are under enormous pressures.

Test yourself

Read the following extract and answer the question that follows.

Vale Karate is a family-run professional karate organisation established and run by Chief Instructor Rob Copeland 6th Dan, Leah Copeland 3rd Dan and secretary Cathy Copeland and based at Vale Karate's Dojo at Barry Leisure Centre.

We aim to make each student's time with Vale Karate enjoyable and beneficial. Vale Karate is:
- a place to meet old friends and make new ones
- a place to improve your fitness and wellbeing, reduce stress and take advantage of the wide array of benefits karate delivers both physically and mentally
- a place to learn the absorbing and challenging art of shotokan and the exciting sport of karate.

We offer a host of traditional classes that are stepping stones towards a fulfilling and successful karate career.

(www.valekarate.com/about-us)

How does the writer show that karate is an enjoyable and beneficial sport?

You should comment on:
- what he says
- his use of language and tone
- the structure of the text.

(10 marks)

Answers on p. 101

How to prepare for the exam

Read a short article online or in a newspaper. As you read, ask yourself:
- What is the main topic of this article?
- Why is it structured in this way?
- What effects do the language choices have on you?
- What sort of tone has the writer used?

Component 2, QA3 Making sense of information

What this question involves

This question will usually be based on the second text and divided into smaller parts, worth 1 or 2 marks each. You will have to find a detail in the text for each.

You are most likely to be asked to find explicit information, although you may be asked to work out the meaning of something from its use in the extract.

Timing

You should re-read the second text to refresh your understanding of it. There are 3 marks for this question, so aim to spend about 3–4 minutes answering it.

What the examiner is looking for

The details you find need to be:
● relevant to the question.

Or, if you are putting an idea into your own words:
● proven by the source.

In this unit you will revise how to:
● deduce the meaning of unfamiliar words
● find the information you need.

The question will tell you very clearly which text you should be looking at, so read the instructions carefully.

Task

As this question will be on a nineteenth-century text, you may be unfamiliar with some of the language that is used. However, the text will still be accessible to you if you read it slowly and carefully.

1 Read the following sentences. Show your understanding of the unfamiliar words by rephrasing the underlined sections in your own words.
   For example: 'I did not apologise for **entreating my neighbours** for help' – 'begging my neighbours.'
   a He <u>endeavoured</u> to solve the problem –
   b Mrs Coulthard promised to <u>furnish</u> the police with the information –
   c You should not enter the classroom <u>unbidden</u>, but wait until you are asked –
   d He had a <u>most prodigious</u> amount of money –
   Answers:
   a **tried** to solve
   b **give** the police the information
   c **without being asked**
   d a lot

prefix: a prefix is added to the start of a word to change its meaning; for example, **un**likely, **dis**appear

suffix: a suffix is added to the end of a word; these often change the word class; for example, child**ish** (changes the noun to an adjective) like**able** (changes the verb to an adjective)

Tasks

Read the following extract in which the author, Charles Dickens, gives an account of a visit he made to Newgate prison in London in 1836, in which he describes the conditions he found there. Answer the questions that follow.

> We entered the first cell. It was a stone dungeon, eight feet long by six wide, with a bench at the upper end, under which were a common rug, a bible, and prayer-book. An iron candlestick was fixed into the wall at the side; and a small high window in the back admitted as much air and light as could struggle in between a double row of heavy, crossed iron bars. It contained no other furniture of any description.

(Extract from *Sketches by Boz*, Charles Dickens, 1836)

1 What are the measurements of the prison cell? (1 mark)
2 What are conditions like in the cell? (2 marks)
Answers:
○ eight feet long by six wide
○ basic – just a bench, rug, bible, prayer-book and iron candlestick; it 'contained no other furniture'; it's dark as the window is 'small' and 'high' with 'heavy, crossed iron bars'

Exam tip

Look out for more of a range of adverbs of degree in nineteenth-century texts than we use today. An adverb of degree is a word that conveys the extent of something; for example, 'very', 'extremely', 'some'. Nineteenth-century texts tend to use adverbs such as 'considerably', 'heartily', 'greatly', or a superlative: *most* saddened. The effect is often that a nineteenth-century text may sound more dramatic in conveying emotions.

Test yourself

TESTED

Read the extract below, written in 1812, in which the patient gives an account of preparations for her operation without anaesthetic. Answer the questions that follow.

> My distress was, I suppose, apparent, for Mr Dubois himself spoke soothingly. 'Can *you*,' I cried, 'feel my apprehension for an operation that, to *you*, must seem so trivial?' – 'Trivial?' he repeated – taking up a bit of paper, which he tore, unconsciously, into a million of pieces, '*Yes – it's a small thing – but,*' he stammered, and could not go on. No one else attempted to speak, and I saw even Mr Dubois grow agitated, while Dr Larry kept always aloof, yet a glance showed me he was pale as ashes. Every thing convinced me danger was hovering about me, but that this experiment could alone save me from its laws. I climbed, therefore, unbidden, on to the bedstead – and Mr Dubois placed me upon the mattress and spread a cambric handkerchief upon my face.

('Account from Paris of a Terrible Operation, 1812', Fanny Burney, Letter to Esther Burney, March 22–June 1812)

1 What two words show you that the patient is nervous and upset? (2 marks)
2 What does the patient climb on to in order to get ready for the operation? (1 mark)

Answers on p. 101

How to prepare for the exam

Find out the meaning of the following words and expressions that were used more frequently in the nineteenth century than today: 'acclamation', 'affront', 'by and by', 'countenance', 'comely', 'covert', 'multitude', 'relish', 'risible'.

Component 2, QA4 Forming opinions

What this question involves

This question is likely to ask you what you think and feel about an aspect of the text or how successful the writer is in describing a particular event or experience.

Although the wording of this question is different to the evaluation task in Component 1, its aims are similar. You will still need to consider how the writer conveys information and analyse how successful he or she is in doing this by looking at the techniques that are used.

This question is worth 10 marks.

Timing

You will already have read the extract but you will need to re-read the specified lines or, in some cases, the whole extract again. There are 10 marks for this question so aim to spend about 12 minutes answering it.

What the examiner is looking for

The examiner is looking for evidence that you can:
- understand the writer's feelings, views or account of an experience
- form an opinion on these
- assess how successfully the writer conveys ideas by analysing the effect of language and techniques
- support what you say with appropriate textual references.

In this unit you will revise how to:
- engage with a writer's view or account
- analyse techniques
- express your opinion clearly.

> **Typical mistakes**
>
> Although the question may ask what you think or feel, don't be tempted to just give a simple personal response. You need to assess the writer's techniques and find evidence to support what you say.

Tasks

The extract below was used in the previous unit. Re-read this and start to think about *how* the writer creates a tense atmosphere.

she's upt →
tries to offer comfort →
ellipsis shows his nerves
awkward silence →
senses danger →

her distress is obvious
'cried' suggests fear
echoes her words
nervous actions
worried
simile shows his nerves
decides to get on with it /brave

My distress was, I suppose, apparent, for Mr Dubois himself spoke soothingly. 'Can *you*,' I cried, 'feel my apprehension for an operation that, to *you*, must seem so trivial?' – 'Trivial?'he repeated – taking up a bit of paper, which he tore, unconsciously, into a million of pieces, '*Yes* – *it's a small thing– but*,' he stammered, and could not go on. No one else attempted to speak, and I saw even Mr Dubois grow agitated, while Dr Larry kept always aloof, yet a glance showed me he was pale as ashes. Every thing convinced me danger was hovering about me, but that this experiment could alone save me from its laws. I climbed, therefore, unbidden, on to the bedstead—and Mr Dubois placed me upon the mattress and spread a cambric handkerchief upon my face.

('Account from Paris of a Terrible Operation, 1812', Fanny Burney, Letter to Esther Burney, March 22–June 1812)

1 How successful do you think the writer is in describing the tense
atmosphere in the operating theatre?   (10 marks)
You should comment on:
○ what happens
○ how the writer describes it.
You must refer to the text to support your comments.

Use the sentence starters and prompts below to help guide you through
your answer. You could use this structure when you write your answer.

Point	The tense atmosphere is conveyed clearly through the use of the word,
Evidence (find a quote)	
Explanation	This suggests that ...
Point	The atmosphere is further emphasised in the phrase,
Evidence	
Explanation (find a quote)	which creates a sense of ...

2 Now write the rest of your response. The question is worth 10 marks,
so you will need to use a **P**oint – **E**vidence – **E**xplanation structure at
least three more times.

Mark scheme

Grade	Descriptors
9	A subtle evaluation of how the writer conveys the tense atmosphere, supported by a wide range of purposeful textual references. Sophisticated and articulate consideration of whether techniques are successful in conveying this.
7, 8	A perceptive evaluation of how the writer conveys the tense atmosphere, supported by precise textual references. Coherent consideration of the success of techniques.
5, 6	Gives a thoughtful evaluation of the writer's use of language and techniques in conveying a tense atmosphere, supported by well-selected textual references.
4	Starts to consider the writer's techniques, supported by relevant quotations.
3	Awareness of some techniques, supported by straightforward evidence.
1, 2	Gives a simple personal opinion with use of superficial evidence.

Assessment comment

It can be difficult to assess your own work but, as a guide, if you have
used a **P**oint – **E**vidence – **E**xplanation structure, ensured that each of
your points are focused on the question's demands and have selected
precise evidence from the text, you should have done well.

Purpose   REVISED ☐

To assess how successful the writer is in conveying an experience or
opinion, it is helpful for you to consider the purpose of the text. The
purpose is simply the writer's reason for producing the text. Once you
have identified this, you can decide to what extent he or she achieves
their aims.

The aim of the texts you are given in Component 2 will be to either
inform, **persuade** *or* **advise**.

To help you identify which it is, think about what the writer wants you to do with this text. If it is just to learn more about something, it is an **informative** text. If it calls upon you to do something as a result of reading, such as buy a product, give to charity or sign up for something, it is a **persuasive** text. If it is giving recommendations for action or behaviour, it is an **advice** text.

Task

1 Decide whether the purpose of the following texts is to inform, persuade or advise. Identify the language and techniques used that led you to identify each.

Text A

Before I describe a visit of my own to a prison Ragged School, and urge the readers of this letter for God's sake to visit one themselves, and think of it (which is my main object), let me say, that I know the prisons of London well, and that the children in them are enough to break the heart and hope of any man.

(*The Daily News*, letter written by Charles Dickens, 4 February 1846)

Text B

Every little girl, before she is twelve years old, should know how to cut and make a shirt with perfect accuracy and neatness.

(*The Little Girl's Own Book*, Lydia Maria Francis Child and Eliza Leslie, 1847)

Text C

As early as six o'clock, the space opposite Charing Cross and Trafalgar Square was crowded to excess by persons of every rank and description, from the rich citizen to the poor mechanic, all anxious to catch a glimpse of and to show their loyalty to England's queen.

(*Hereford Times*, 30 June 1838, British Newspaper Archive)

Answers:

Text A: Persuasive. Strong verb – 'urge'. Exhortation – 'For God's sake'. **Imperative** – 'visit one', 'think of it'. States aim – 'which is my main object'. Has experience – 'I know the prisons of London well' to convince. Emotive language – 'break the heart and hope of any man'.

Text B: Advises. Inclusive – 'every'. Fact – 'before she is twelve years old'. Strong verbs – 'should know'. States objective – 'cut and make a shirt'. Adjective and noun stress the required talent – 'perfect accuracy'.

Text C: Informative. Establishes when – 'six o'clock'. Establishes where – 'opposite Charing Cross and Trafalgar Square'. Past tense recounts event – 'was crowded'. Use of opposites informs reader about the crowd – 'every rank and description', 'rich citizen to the poor mechanic'. Feelings – 'anxious'. Qualities – 'loyalty'. Establishes who – 'England's queen'. Details shows us the text aims to inform.

Task

In completing the previous exercise, you considered the writer's language choices, and also the techniques that were used.

You may have noticed the imperatives in Text A, such as 'visit one' and 'think of it'. The writer also draws on personal experience to illustrate that they know what they are writing about, 'I know the prisons of

> **Exam tip**
>
> Note that writers who write to **inform** or **advise** may also entertain, explain or describe in order to inform or make recommendations. Writers who **persuade** may also do this, before asking you to sign up to or buy something. To identify the text, look at what it wants you to do by the end.

> **imperative**: a command or instruction

London well'. The writer of Text B uses facts – 'twelve years old' – in order to advise specifically and Text C uses opposites in 'rich citizen to the poor mechanic' to encompass a range of examples.

Each of these techniques helps the writer to achieve their aims.

1 Read the following informative text and identify the techniques that the writer uses. What is the effect of each of these?

Look for:
○ emotive language
○ dramatic punctuation (questions, exclamations or **ellipsis**)
○ facts and figures
○ personal experience
○ **comparatives** and superlatives
○ **personal pronouns**
○ **parallel structure**

I find myself confined to the house for inordinate amounts of time. This is due to the onset of a most vexing condition, from which I have suffered for ten long years but is far worse of late. How can I describe this most extreme of feelings? The condition results in a tightening of the throat and a shortness of the breath that is quite acute! It has long caused me great concern and even, I admit, resulted in bouts of dark depression, from which I have sometimes felt that I would not recover. Yet of late, whenever I find myself growing melancholy, I sit by an open casement. It is infinitely more pleasant to take the afternoon air from the garden than breathe the dense stench of a closed room.

Answers:
○ Emotive language: 'inordinate amounts', 'most vexing', 'suffered', 'extreme', 'great concern', 'dark depression'.
○ Facts and figures: 'ten long years'.
○ Personal experience: the account of the illness.
○ Personal pronouns: '*I* find myself,' '*I* have suffered,' 'caused *me*'.
○ Dramatic punctuation: 'How can I describe this most extreme of feelings?', 'quite acute!'
○ Parallel structure: 'to take the afternoon air from the garden than breathe the dense stench of a closed room'.
○ Comparatives: 'worse', 'more pleasant'.
○ Superlatives: 'most vexing', 'most extreme'.

Tasks

You should also consider the structure of the texts.

1 An informative text will usually:
○ state a topic
○ give a series of steps or details about the topic
○ give an overview or summary of the topic.
What is successful about structuring an informative text this way?

2 A persuasive text will usually:
○ state the writer's opinion
○ find evidence to support this opinion
○ persuade the reader to adopt this opinion.
What is successful about structuring a persuasive text this way?

3 An advisory text will usually:
○ state a topic
○ give the consequences of certain behaviour
○ explain the steps to prevent problems
○ give an overview of the resolution.
What is successful about structuring an advisory text this way?

---

personal pronoun: a word that replaces the noun: 'he', 'she', 'we', 'they', 'it'

ellipsis: three dots (…) to show a missing piece of text or a pause for effect

parallel structures: using the same pattern of words to show the equal importance of ideas; for example, 'I would rather play computer games than revise GCSE papers'

hyperbole: an exaggerated statement that is not meant to be taken literally

comparative: comparatives compare two options; for example, 'Rugby is a better game than American football'

Exam tip

Nineteenth-century prose is often quite elaborate. Complex sentences are common, with use of many clauses. Often, the main clause (the main part of the sentence, that could stand alone grammatically) is at the end of the sentence. The reader has to wait until they reach this to understand the main point.

Typical mistakes

Simple comments on what the text looks like will not gain you many marks. Do not count paragraphs, guess at font size or say that a title is 'big and bold'. Instead, comment on the specific effects of the writer's language choices and the techniques used.

Answers:

1 Firstly, the topic is made clear. The steps give more detail and the overview clarifies the most important features.

2 Firstly, a certain point of view is put forward, the argument is strengthened through the evidence that follows, then, once the reader has been drawn into the argument, their agreement or sympathy is appealed to.

3 Firstly, the reader identifies the topic. They are warned of unwanted consequences, then learn how to avoid them, and are left with the final message.

Test yourself

TESTED

Now answer the question:

What do you think and feel about the prisoner's situation?

You should comment on:
- the conditions in the prison
- how the prisoner's thoughts and feelings are conveyed.

(10 marks)

Answers on p. 101

How to prepare for the exam

Re-read one of the nineteenth-century extracts either in this unit or in the previous one for Component 2, Question A3. Identify the use and effect of the writer's language and techniques, and how the structure of the extract helps to make the text more memorable.

Component 2, QA5 Finding information from two texts

What this question involves

This question is likely to be based on both texts. It will ask you to find information from both and to put this information together. You may be asked what impression the texts create of an experience or topic.

The question is likely to ask you to find implicit information, so you need to locate points, then deduce what these show you about the subject.

This question is worth 4 marks.

Timing

You will need to skim-read both texts to find relevant information. You will then need to put it together in your answer. There are 4 marks for this question, so aim to spend about 5 minutes answering it.

What the examiner is looking for

The examiner is hoping that you will have:
● selected evidence from both texts
● put this evidence together in a focused answer.

In this unit you will revise:
● how to select the best evidence
● how to put it together in a cohesive response.

Tasks

This question is worth 4 marks, so you will need to be focused and succinct.

A good rule is to find two pieces of evidence from the first text and two from the second. Keep the question in mind as you read the extracts.

Read the extracts below.

The birth of Princess Charlotte

The Lindo Wing has been the focus of hundreds of cameras around the world for weeks, and now it is becoming a tourist attraction in its own right. Tourists and royal fans have started a craze by posing for selfies on the steps outside the private maternity wing of St Mary's Hospital in Paddington. Some people have been spotted substituting the royal baby for bags – and even pets, for that *authentic* look!

(*Telegraph*, 5 May 2015)

The Coronation of Queen Victoria

At ten minutes past 11 o'clock, Her Majesty in the Royal State carriage passed Charing Cross. At this moment, the waving of handkerchiefs from every balcony and window, and the loud huzzas and demonstrations of loyalty from the congregated thousands below, portrayed a scene which it is impossible for pen to describe. Her Majesty appeared highly delighted, and repeatedly bowed in the most condescending manner. Upon the Royal Carriage arriving at the Admiralty, the acclamations of the assembled multitude were renewed.

(*Hereford Times*, 30 June 1838, British Newspaper Archive)

1 Underline two pieces of evidence from the first text and two from the second that you could use to answer the question:
Explain how people react towards the royal family. (4 marks)
Both texts will be linked through their topic, so you are more likely to be asked a question about the similar way they present this. However, as the texts will have been written at least one hundred years apart, you may be asked about the different way they present a topic or experience.

2 Now write your answer in full to the question:
Using information from both texts, explain how people react towards the royal family. (4 marks)
Answer: Both texts are about people's excited reactions towards the royal family.
Evidence from the first text. Any two from:
○ the Lindo Wing is the focus of hundreds of cameras
○ it's become a tourist attraction
○ fans are posing for selfies
○ people are holding bags and pets to pretend it's a baby.
Evidence from the second text. Any two from:
○ people were waving handkerchiefs (from balconies and windows)
○ there was cheering ('loud huzzas')
○ demonstrations of loyalty from the crowd
○ the cheers ('acclamations') of the crowd began again when the queen bowed.
Award 1 mark for each, up to a maximum of 4.

A clear way to start your answer is by beginning with a sentence which summarises both texts' approach to the topic in the question. For example, in two texts about skiing, you could start: 'Both texts show the difficulties of undertaking a winter sport.'

Exam tip

Structure your answer clearly by using linking phrases, such as 'also', 'similarly', 'likewise'.

Component 2, QA5 Finding information from two texts

TESTED ☐

Test yourself

Read the following texts and answer the question:

Using information from both texts, what effects can result from saying unkind things about other people? (4 marks)

a **Against deceptive remarks and representations**

Guard against duplicity. Never volunteer unnecessarily in speaking ill of anybody. In no case allow yourself to make an unfavourable representation of a character, unless you have ample evidence that it is in accordant with truth. By neglecting to observe this suggestion, you may irretrievably injure an innocent person, and procure for yourself an undesirable name.

(*The Lady's Guide to Perfect Gentility, in Manners, Dress and Conversation,* Emily Thornwell, 1857)

b **Why do people troll on the internet?**

Every internet troll will excuse their behaviour in different ways but, behind their shiny computer and screen name, they are usually depressed, jealous and cowardly people who momentarily feel stronger through posting unpleasant messages online. This strength is short-lived, however. Back in the real world, they remain dissatisfied and ultimately make themselves unhappy in the secret knowledge of what they've done.

Answers on p. 102

How to prepare for the exam

As you will need to combine ideas from two texts for both Question A5 and Question A6 in Component 2, it is worth learning linking words and phrases.
● For similar ideas, learn: 'also', 'similarly', 'likewise', 'both writers show that …'.
● For different ideas, learn: 'by contrast', 'although', 'conversely'.

WJEC Eduqas GCSE (9–1) English Language   71

Component 2, QA6 Comparing writers' ideas

What this question involves

You will usually be asked to compare how the writers feel about the topics of their texts or an experience and how they communicate this to the reader. You will need to move between the texts, cross-referencing the effects of language and technique.

This question is worth 10 marks.

Timing

This is arguably the most challenging question in Section A of Component 2. It is worth 10 marks. As you have to put together information from two texts and compare this, aim to spend about 12–14 minutes answering.

What the examiner is looking for

The examiner is looking for evidence that you can:
● identify the writers' attitudes towards the topic of their texts
● analyse how they present these attitudes
● compare these attitudes and how they are conveyed.

In this unit you will revise how to:
● identify the approach to a topic or experience
● analyse the language and techniques used
● compare writers' ideas and perspectives.

This type of question requires you to **synthesise** ideas. This means that you must use information from both texts and combine this in order to write your answer.

> **synthesis**: combining information to form a whole

To synthesise information, you need to:
● understand the demands of the question
● find the information you need in the first text
● find the information you need in the second text
● combine this information to form your answer.

It is up to you whether you would prefer to write about all the evidence you need from the first text, then all the evidence you need from the second text, then compare them at the end, *or* compare the texts back and forth as you write your answer.

The key word is 'compare' and you may find that you can do more of this if you compare as you go, rather than at the end when you run the risk of running out of time, or just repeating the earlier part of your answer.

Task

Read the following extracts and find some of the techniques that you practised analysing in the earlier tasks for Component 2, Question 4.

Look for:
● emotive language
● questions

- facts and figures
- exclamations
- personal experience
- the tone of the texts
- personal pronouns
- the structure of the texts

These techniques are *not* a checklist and will not be in every examination text. They are a starting point so that you have some ideas of what to look for.

Text A

Why does gender-stereotyped toy marketing matter?

How toys are labelled and displayed affects consumers' buying habits. Many people feel uncomfortable buying a boy a pink toy or a girl a toy labelled as 'for boys'. Other buyers may simply be unaware of the restricted choices they are offered. They may not notice that science kits and construction toys are missing from the 'girls' section, or art & crafts and kitchen toys from the 'boys'. If they're never offered the chance, a child may never find out if they enjoy a certain toy or style of play. Children are taking in these messages about what girls and boys are 'supposed to like'. They are looking for patterns and social rules and absorb the gender rule, 'This is for boys and that is for girls.' These rigid boundaries turn children away from their true preferences.

(http://lettoysbetoys.org.uk/why-it-matters)

Text B

There is no accomplishment of any kind more desirable for a woman than neatness and skill in the use of a needle. To some, it is an employment not only useful, but absolutely necessary, and it furnishes a tasteful necessity for all. Every little girl, before she is twelve years old, should know how to cut and make a shirt with perfect accuracy and neatness. I have seen young ladies make sleeves and sew them into the shirt, before the wristbands were put on! I have never had a high opinion of little girls who frequently say, 'I don't care', or, 'What matter is it?' The fact is, it is a great deal of consequence. Little girls who really wish to learn, will soon find some kind sister, or aunt, or grandmother, who will gladly teach them.

(*The Little Girl's Own Book*, Lydia Maria Francis Child and Eliza Leslie, 1847)

> **Typical mistakes**
>
> Do not say what techniques are *not* used, or suggest what the writer could have included instead. Analyse what *is* there!

> **Exam tip**
>
> You may wish to use some of the information and quotes that you have already used to answer earlier questions. Although you should not just copy out what you said in your other answers, it is perfectly acceptable to use some of the same quotes and ideas if they are relevant.

Tasks

Consider the following question:

Both of these texts are about children's activities. Compare:
- the writer's attitudes to children's activities
- how they make their views clear to the reader.

You must use the text to support your comments and make it clear which text you are referring to.

Read these extracts from student responses. The first student is just 'spotting' techniques, whereas the second is looking at the effect of the writers' use of language and techniques and comparing this.

This is how a Grade 3 student began:

unclear which text is being referred to

could strengthen with a direct quote

should not suggest what the writer could have done

having a go at **P**oint – **E**vidence – **E**xplanation

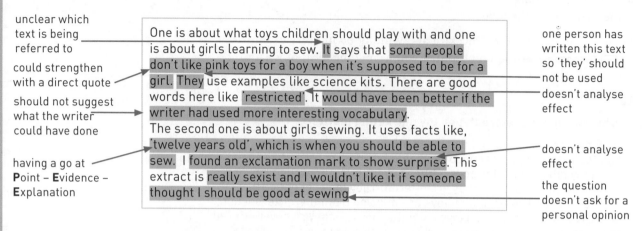

One is about what toys children should play with and one is about girls learning to sew. It says that some people don't like pink toys for a boy when it's supposed to be for a girl. They use examples like science kits. There are good words here like 'restricted'. It would have been better if the writer had used more interesting vocabulary.
The second one is about girls sewing. It uses facts like, 'twelve years old', which is when you should be able to sew. I found an exclamation mark to show surprise. This extract is really sexist and I wouldn't like it if someone thought I should be good at sewing.

one person has written this text so 'they' should not be used

doesn't analyse effect

doesn't analyse effect

the question doesn't ask for a personal opinion

This is how a Grade 9 student began:

overview of topic

understands structure

clearly identifies which text is being dealt with

clever cross-reference of ideas

Both texts look at different approaches to gender-appropriate activities. The heading of Text A asks, 'Why does gender-stereotyped toy marketing matter?' and the question used immediately implies that it does matter and that the article will explain why. By contrast, Text B is titled, 'The Little Girl's Own Book', which immediately suggests that the advice that follows will only be for females, insinuating that there is a certain way they should behave. Text A identifies that different toys are marketed to boys and girls and argues that this is fundamentally wrong as it can make people 'uncomfortable'. This suggests that gender rules are so rigid that buyers feel like they're breaking some sort of unspoken law if they dare to buy something that doesn't fit the stereotype. Text B reinforces exactly the kind of stereotypes that Text A rejects, by claiming that 'neatness and skill' in sewing is absolutely necessary for a woman.

embeds quotation

moves between texts
comments on structure

precise quotation

perceptive discussion of ideas

1 When you are moving between the texts, use some of the vocabulary you learned in the previous unit.
   ○ For similar ideas, use: 'also', 'similarly', 'likewise', 'both writers show that …'.
   ○ For different ideas, use: 'by contrast', 'although', 'conversely'.
2 Continue the Grade 9 answer. You would have about 12–14 minutes for this question in total, so aim to spend about 7 more minutes completing it.

Mark scheme

Grade	Descriptors
9	Makes subtle and sustained comparisons and contrasts.
	Exacting analysis of the writers' use of language and techniques.
	Uses purposeful textual references.
7, 8	Careful and perceptive comparisons and contrasts.
	Close analysis of the writers' use of language and techniques.
	Uses precise textual references.
5, 6	Detailed comparisons and contrasts.
	Thoughtful analysis of the writers' use of language and techniques.
	Uses well-selected textual references.
4	Makes some comparisons between attitudes and ideas.
	Starts to look at the writers' techniques.
	Some relevant quotations are used.
3	Shows that the writers' attitudes are different.
	Some awareness of the writers' language choices and techniques.
	Straightforward quotations.
1, 2	Identifies basic similarities and/or differences.
	Finds simple evidence to support.

> **Exam tip**
>
> As this is an English exam, it is worth getting your grammar right. When you compare two texts, you should use comparatives, not superlatives. You can say which text was the 'better' *or* the 'more' effective. (Do not say, the 'best' text or the 'most' effective, as superlatives are only used for three or more things.)

Task

If Question 6 asks you to compare the writers' attitudes towards a topic or experience, you will need to identify *what* their opinions are before you can compare them and analyse *how* they are conveyed.

Read the following texts.

Decide how the writer feels about marriage in each case.

Text A

You ought never to marry any person who is not able to afford you a decent and immediate support. In my experience, I have witnessed the long years of patient misery and dependence which fine women have endured from rushing into matrimonial connections without sufficient reflection. Look ahead and consider the future, and act wisely in this particular.

('Famous American Belles of the Nineteenth Century',
Virginia Tatnall Peacock, 1901)

Text B

Ways to tell you're with the person you should marry

While it's not pleasant to think about the worst of the worst that life can throw at you, when considering whether or not you're with the person to marry, it can be useful to consider the darker side of life and how you imagine the two of you might fair through it together. Another factor is that while looks, wealth and charisma are what initially reels someone in, what makes someone stay for the long-term is accepting your partner's idiosyncrasies. Finally, a great way to determine if you're ready to tie the knot is by asking yourself if your partner feels like a true friend.

(https://mic.com/articles/110744/6-ways-to-tell-you-re-with-the-person-you-should-marry-according-to-science#.qeSkL1BrM)

1 Complete the table by finding a quote and commenting on what it shows you about each writer's attitude towards marriage. The first row has been completed for you.

The writers' attitudes to marriage		
	Text A	**Text B**
Quote	'long years of patient misery'	'accepting your partner's idiosyncrasies'
What this shows	Marriage can be miserable if you rush into it	Marriage isn't about changing someone
Quote		
What this shows		
Quote		
What this shows		

You may have considered:

● Text A: 'Look ahead' – you should think about the future; 'act wisely' – approach marriage thoughtfully
● Text B: 'consider the darker side of life' – a marriage should get through the difficult times; 'a true friend' – marriage is about companionship.

Tasks

1 Read the following text about a doctor who can calm crying babies.
How does the writer feel about the method the doctor uses?
Look particularly at the highlighted words to help you identify the writer's feelings.

Text A

the writer isn't expecting this technique →

It's not surprising then that paediatrician Robert Hamilton has seen a lot of crying babies. What's more unexpected is his unusual technique for calming them down, which, according to the video, works surprisingly fast.

the writer finds this technique strange

suggests he wouldn't have believed it if he hadn't seen it

he's amazed at the quick effect →

2 Now read the second text about comforting crying babies.
How does the writer feel about the methods described?
Look at the highlighted words to help you identify the writer's feelings.

Text B

objects to these methods → only negative results are given → suggests discomfort →

not in favour of acting like this

strong verb suggests criticism

an unpleasant quality suggests violent actions

choice of adverb suggests disapproval

simile shows an extreme action

All loud noises and violent motions should be avoided. They pain an infant's senses and distract his faculties. I have seen impatient nurses thrust a glaring candle before the eyes of a fretful babe, or drum violently on the table, or rock the cradle like an earthquake.

The highlighted words and phrases will have helped you to identify how the writers feel about the topic of calming crying babies.

You would use this highlighted vocabulary to support the points you make in your answer. You can also use the words and phrases about tone that you practised in the section on Component 2, Question 2. For example: 'serious', 'light-hearted', 'approving', 'scornful'.

Task

1 Read the following vocabulary lists that you could use to describe the tone of a text. Decide which you would use to describe each writer's feelings in the two extracts you have just read.

   ○ **Positive:** approves of, commends, writes positively about.
   ○ **Negative:** attacks, scorns, disparages, criticises.

   To structure your answer, a useful plan is to:

   ○ write a summarising sentence that links the topic of the texts
   ○ find words and phrases in Text A that help you identify the writer's attitude
   ○ use these to analyse *how* the writer's attitude is conveyed
   ○ find words and phrases in Text B that help you identify the writer's attitude
   ○ use these to analyse *how* the writer's attitude is conveyed
   ○ construct your answer by using linking phrases, such as 'similarly', 'likewise' or 'by contrast', 'conversely'.

Test yourself

TESTED ☐

Re-read the texts about how to calm a baby, then, using the annotations, suggested vocabulary and structure ideas given, write a full answer of your own to this question:

Both of these texts are about the methods for calming crying babies.

Compare:
a how the writers feel about these methods
b how they make their views clear to the reader.

(10 marks)

Answers on p. 102

How to prepare for the exam

Use the internet to find similar articles about a topic that interests you, such as music, films or a particular hobby. It is difficult to find nineteenth-century non-fiction texts, but it will still be useful to practise with two modern articles. Identify the writer's attitudes in each, find vocabulary and techniques that helped you to understand these attitudes, and compare how the writers use their techniques.

Component 2, Section B Transactional and persuasive writing

What this question involves

There will be two compulsory writing tasks, which means you must answer both questions. The questions are likely to be formal writing tasks, such as an article, formal letter, report, speech, leaflet or review. You will need to show that you can write effectively for different purposes and audiences, with careful use of grammar, punctuation and spelling.

Each question is worth 20 marks, with 12 marks awarded for the content and organisation of your answer, and 8 marks for vocabulary, sentence structure, spelling and punctuation. Section B is out of a total of 40 for both tasks.

You should aim to write about 300–400 words for *each* answer.

> **transactional writing**: communicates ideas by informing or persuading, in the form of articles, letters, reports, speeches, reviews or leaflets

Timing

You should spend 30 minutes on each question, with 5 minutes spent on planning and 25 minutes writing each time. Spend an hour on Section B altogether.

What the examiner is looking for

The examiner is looking for evidence that you can:
● write well for the appropriate purpose and audience of each task
● organise your answer clearly
● use grammar, punctuation and spelling carefully.

In this unit you will revise how to:
● identify the correct purpose and audience for your answer
● write in the correct format
● use the right tone and register for the task.

> **Typical mistakes**
>
> Do not waste time counting your words or write how many you've done so far on your answer. With average-sized writing, 400 words is about 1¼ A4 sides.

Purpose, audience and format

REVISED

The **purpose** is the reason for writing the piece, such as to inform, persuade or advise. The question will state the purpose of your task, and the examiner will be looking that you are confident in writing for the reason given.

You may wish to review the section on 'purpose' in Component 2, Question A4 unit of this book. Remember:
● an **informative** text gives you information
● a **persuasive** text calls upon you to do something as a result of reading
● an **advisory** text guides and gives recommendations.

The **audience** for your task is likely to be stated, such as writing an article for your school magazine (where your audience is your own age group), a letter to a potential employer, or a guide for primary school students. You will need to choose the correct language and tone for the intended audience.

The **form** is the type of task, such as an article, letter or guide.

Tasks

Identify the purpose, audience and format of each of these tasks.

form = report ⎯⎯ For example: Write a **report** for the headteacher ⟵⎯⎯ audience = the headteacher
suggesting ways to save energy at school. ⟵⎯⎯ purpose = advice

1 A proposal has been made to set aside a graffiti wall in your school for an art project. Write an article for your school magazine, arguing in favour of or against this idea.
2 Write a letter to the editor of your local newspaper, giving your views on the facilities for young people in your town.
3 Write a guide aimed at parents, advising them how to help their teenage children deal with examination stress.

Answers:
1 Form = article; audience = students; purpose = to persuade.
2 Form = letter; audience = editor and those reading the newspaper; purpose = to give your views.
3 Form = guide; audience = parents; purpose = to advise.

Planning

REVISED ☐

Once you have identified the form, audience and purpose of your task, you can start planning. Aim to spend about 3–5 minutes planning, leaving you with 25 minutes to write your answer.

Your answer should:
● have a logical structure
● include a range of suitable techniques (strong words, facts, examples)
● avoid repeating ideas
● have an engaging opening and memorable ending.

Planning steps:
● Create a spider diagram of ideas.
● Put these in order and think how you'll link them.
● Develop these ideas.
● Think of a heading and strong opening sentence.

Task

1 Work through the bullet points above to help you plan an answer to the task:
Write a leaflet for your school's physical education department, encouraging students to exercise more.

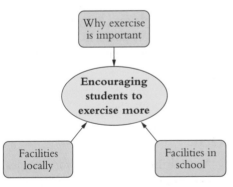

Putting ideas in order and linking them

1 Why exercise is important.
So where can we go to do this?

↓

2 Facilities in school.
What if we want a new challenge?

↓

3 Facilities locally

Developing these ideas

Can you add more ideas to each of your three main headings for this task?

As you add ideas, think of effective techniques that you could use in each.
For example:

1 Why exercise is important:
  ○ Keeps you healthy. Use personal pronouns. '*You* will feel better if
    you …'
  ○ Controls weight. Facts. Childhood obesity at highest level in UK.
    Nearly 20 per cent of teens obese.
  ○ Improves mood. Quote from student supporting this.
  ○ Gives you energy. Examples.

A heading and strong opening sentence

As the task in this case is to write a leaflet, you will need an engaging
heading.

Effective headings and sub-headings can use:
● statements
● rhetorical questions
● figurative language
● rhymes
● alliteration.

Identify which of these five techniques above are used in the following
examples.
1 Out of the frying pan, into the fire.
2 Top Tips for Taxing Tests.
3 An apple a day no longer pays.
4 UK teenagers perform well in new GCSEs.
5 How can we teach our young people manners?

Answers:

1 figurative language   **2** alliteration   **3** rhyme   **4** statement   **5** rhetorical question

Task

1 Now think of a heading for your leaflet encouraging students to
exercise more. Also think of a sub-heading for each of the three main
ideas of your leaflet. Try to use a different technique each time.

Tasks

You are now ready to write the opening sentence of your leaflet. You
might decide to begin with:

- a general statement of the importance of exercise
- a rhetorical question
- a fact.

Read the following two openings from students' leaflets.

> I am going to write a leaflet about exercise. It is really important because you need to keep healthy and this leaflet will show you.

> **Why working out can be wonderful**
>
> With nearly 20 per cent of British teenagers obese, it's clearly time for us to heave ourselves off the sofa, put down that games console and put away the pizza. Not convinced? Well, the benefits of exercise aren't just that it stops your PE teacher from nagging you quite so much.

1 The second example is from a Grade 8 answer. Why is it better than the first?
  Hopefully, you noted the memorable heading, use of a shocking fact, the personal pronoun, 'us', to involve the reader, a rhetorical question and a chatty, friendly tone. In contrast to this, the first response is uninspiring. The beginning – 'I am going to write a leaflet' – is also not how a real leaflet would actually begin.

2 Now write the opening sentences of your leaflet about encouraging students to exercise more.

Tasks

You may also wish to plan an ending at this stage. Effective endings:
- are memorable
- are linked to the task's original aims
- pick up on an idea used at the beginning.

Before you write your ending, consider what the main aim of your leaflet is and what you hope the reader will do as a result of it; in this case, take more exercise. This is the message that you need to end with so that you have fulfilled the aims of the task.

Read the following two endings from students' leaflets.

> I hope you have enjoyed this leaflet and that you take more exercise.

> So, now that the indent of your inert body is gone from your sofa and your games console has had a rest, you've probably earned a slice or two of pizza. With regular involvement in any of the activities outlined here, you'll be fighting fit in no time. So, what are you waiting for?

1 Which is from a Grade 3 response and which is from a Grade 8?
  Answer: The Grade 8 response is the second. Why is it better than the first?
  You probably picked up on the links to the ideas about the sofa, games console and pizza in the student's opening, the reminder that the aim of the leaflet is to undertake exercise and the final, rhetorical question to inspire readers.

2 Now write the ending of your leaflet about encouraging students to exercise more.

Task

1 Now you have planned your ideas for this task, look at the mark scheme below and consider in which grade your plan best fits. If you feel that it would not score highly, return to your plan and make some changes. You may need to add more ideas or write a stronger beginning.

Mark scheme

Grade	Descriptors
9	Purpose, audience and format is perfectly matched to task. A wide range of ideas are developed with flair and originality. Sophisticated structure and organisation of ideas.
7, 8	Purpose, audience and format is precisely matched to task. A range of ideas are developed with details and are original and creative. Ambitious structure and organisation of ideas.
5, 6	Purpose, audience and format is well matched to task. A range of ideas with examples to support. Clear structure and connected ideas.
4	Clear attempt to match purpose, audience and format to task. Some development of ideas and appropriate examples. Uses paragraphs to organise work and mostly connects ideas.
3	Awareness of purpose, audience and format. Starting to develop ideas, with some examples used. Evidence of organisational techniques.
1, 2	Basic awareness of purpose, audience and format. Simple communication of mostly personal ideas. Basic organisation with few or no paragraphs.

Test yourself

TESTED

Write a detailed plan, then the opening and ending for the following task:

Write a lively article for your school magazine, exploring technology use in your school.

Use the previous mark scheme to help you place your plan in a grade.

Answers on p. 103–104

Articles

REVISED

Purpose

An article informs, entertains and sometimes persuades. You will need to write in a suitable style and with the right tone for your given audience and engage their interest right from the beginning.

Audience

If you are asked to write an article in the exam, the question will probably tell you who your audience are; for example, parents of teenagers, students at your school or local people in your town.
- For an adult audience, use standard English and quite a formal tone.
- For a teenage audience, use standard English but a more informal tone.

Tasks

Read the following sentences. Do you think the tone in each is more appropriate for an adult or teenage audience?

1 So … let's have a think about the best place to do your dreaded homework.
2 Teachers and parents play an essential role in supporting young people.
3 The importance of regular attendance cannot be emphasised enough.
4 If it's friendly advice you want, just pop in to your nearest job centre.

Answers:

1 teenager	2 adults	3 adults	4 teenagers

Format

Use headings, sub-headings and clear paragraphs as the format of your article. Do not write in columns as it makes it difficult for you to judge how much you have written. Avoid drawing pictures. It is not an art exam!

Your first headline should be about the main topic of the article. Subsequent sub-headings show what the content of each main section is about. They also enable readers to skim over the article and identify its main ideas.

Task

Remember that headlines and sub-headings can use statements, rhetorical questions, puns, rhymes and alliteration as possible ideas.

1 Complete the table below with a headline or sub-heading that uses each technique, for the following task:
An article about poor behaviour in UK secondary schools.
Some have already been completed for you.

Headline or sub-heading about poor behaviour in UK secondary schools	
Statement	
Rhetorical question	
Pun or play on words	No method to this madness
Rhyme	Silence the violence
Alliteration	

Ideas could be as follows:
○ Statement – 'Time to put an end to poor behaviour.'
○ Rhetorical question – 'How can we improve behaviour?'
○ Alliteration – 'Ticking timebomb.'

Planning your article

You will need:
● an engaging opening
● a first paragraph that outlines the main points of the topic
● four or five central paragraphs giving more detail about the topic
● a short but decisive ending.

Openings – three effective ways to start are as follows:
● A topic statement. For example: 'Unhealthy eating is a problem in modern society.'
● A specific focus. For example: 'On a warm June morning, a group of students are filing into a large examination hall.'
● A quote. For example: '"I've never found that local leisure centres have adequate facilities," explained Josh Bradley, aged 18.'

Exam tip

A formal tone does not mean a boring tone! It means that you should use standard English rather than slang or text abbreviations, but you can still be light-hearted, chatty in style and humorous if this tone lends itself to the given task.

As people choose to read magazines and newspapers, you are aiming to inform but also to entertain, so use a lively style!

Typical mistakes

Do not use language more suited to an essay. Avoid phrases such as: 'furthermore', 'moreover', 'some people say', 'in conclusion'.

Task

1 Write a starting sentence for the following article writing tasks, trying a different one of the suggested opening techniques for each.
Write an article:
○ for your school magazine about healthy eating during the school day
○ for an online parenting magazine about how to help children with exam stress
○ for your local town paper, about facilities for young people in your area.

The first paragraph – your first paragraph should summarise *who* is affected by the topic, *what* the main points of it are and *where* people might be affected. This paragraph covers the topic in brief, so that readers can gather the main information and decide whether they'd like to learn more by reading the rest of the article.

Task

1 Underline the sections of the following sentences that cover who, what and where.
  a Study leave is nearly upon the students of Stanwell School, so it's time to get organised and think about how to make the best use of your time.
  b It's mobile madness in Park Vale Youth Club, as young people gather to hand in their phones for two hours and try good old-fashioned conversation instead!
  c Local people have been left devastated by the news that Hinkley's Theatre Royal is to close next month.
  Answer **a**:
  ○ Who – students
  ○ What – getting organised for study leave
  ○ Where – Stanwell School
  Answer **b**:
  ○ Who – young people
  ○ What – giving up mobiles for conversation instead
  ○ Where – Park Vale Youth Club
  Answer **c**:
  ○ Who – local people
  ○ What – the theatre is closing
  ○ Where – Hinkley

> **Typical mistakes**
>
> You may wish to use the pronouns 'us' or 'we' if you are writing for a school newspaper, but aim to avoid the word 'I' as an article represents different people's views, not just yours. Use 'A student commented ...' or, 'The headteacher explained ...', not ' A student told *me*.'

Ending your article – the ending of your article should be a short paragraph, summarising the main points and looking at how the main topic of the article may unfold in the future. For example: 'Teachers at the school say that they cannot guarantee that study leave will be extended this year, but they are hoping that this will be a possibility next Summer.'

Aim to read newspaper and magazine articles and online news, so that you become familiar with the structure and ending of articles. Do not end by inviting the reader to phone in (it's not a television programme!) or even to write in.

Tasks

Read the following unsuitable endings. Suggest how each could be improved. For example:
● Weak ending = 'Phone in now to say whether you think the school should ban uniform.'
● Improved = 'The school will hold a consultation in the near future that all students are invited to attend.'

1 Basically, it's disgusting that we are not allowed to use mobile phones in school.
2 Write, email or text us your views about the town music festival.
3 Only healthy food will be served from now on. So, what do you think?

Test yourself

TESTED

Choose *one* of the following article tasks. Each was given earlier in this unit. Aim to write about 300–400 words. Use the mark scheme at the unit's end to assess your work. Write an article:

- for your school magazine about healthy eating during the school day
- for an online parenting magazine about how to help children with exam stress
- for your local town paper, about facilities for young people in your area.

Answers on p. 103–104

Letters

REVISED

Purpose

An informal letter is written to a friend or relative and usually gives information. A formal letter is written to someone you do not know personally or well. Their purpose is to comment on an issue or to bring about a situation, such as applying for a job.

Audience

For a friend, your tone will be friendly and you may wish to include memories of your friendship to lend credibility. If you are asked to write a formal letter, you will probably be required to put forward a viewpoint in a more formal way. You will need to decide what your viewpoint of the given topic is and jot down ideas before you start writing.

Format

You will need to make sure that you set your letter out correctly, as in the following example.

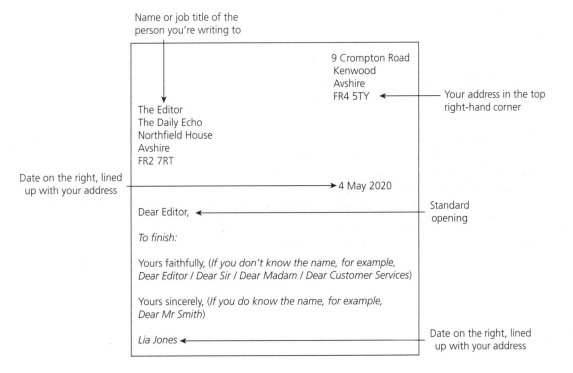

Name or job title of the person you're writing to

9 Crompton Road
Kenwood
Avshire
FR4 5TY

Your address in the top right-hand corner

The Editor
The Daily Echo
Northfield House
Avshire
FR2 7RT

Date on the right, lined up with your address

4 May 2020

Dear Editor,

Standard opening

To finish:

Yours faithfully, (*If you don't know the name, for example, Dear Editor / Dear Sir / Dear Madam / Dear Customer Services*)

Yours sincerely, (*If you do know the name, for example, Dear Mr Smith*)

Lia Jones

Date on the right, lined up with your address

To structure your letter:

- begin with a short paragraph explaining your reasons for writing
- include three or four paragraphs that each put forward a different point
- end by saying what you hope will be the result of your letter
- sign off with the appropriate ending – 'Yours faithfully' or 'Yours sincerely'.

Tasks

Read the following tasks and decide on your point of view about each issue. Write down three main ideas that you would put forward for each.

1 The headteacher has decided to introduce a 'food court' style canteen in your school, with different restaurants serving a wide range of high-quality food. However, the food will be more expensive. Write a letter to the school council, giving your views on this.

2 The government is considering lowering the voting age to 16. Write a letter to your local Member of Parliament, expressing your views on this idea.

Task

1 Read the opening paragraphs of the following two students' letters. Use the annotations to help you understand why each grade was given. You can also refer to the mark scheme at the end of this unit.

Grade 2

Dear Editor

doesn't introduce topic of letter → I think its discusting the way that lots of people behave. I heard a story about someone who kept his dog locked in a cage. You should do something about this because its not right and its cruel so you should do something. It depends though because most people are nice to their pets and it's not much of a problem mostly.

apostrophe is omitted

the editor isn't involved in animal cruelty so the student is giving instructions to the wrong person

spelling error

repetitive

appears to change their mind about the extent of this problem

Grade 8

Dear Editor

explains what led them to write the letter → Having recently read an article about unscrupulous puppy farmers, I feel that I must make local people aware of the risks of buying a dog from an unauthorised breeder.

second paragraph develops topic → It is a shocking fact that the puppies bought from these farms are taken away from their mothers when they are barely six weeks old. Any concerns for welfare, care or appropriate living conditions are all sacrificed to profit. When these dogs are at their most

strong verb → vulnerable, they are snatched from their family and passed to buyers who may not even have seen the puppy with its mother.

ambitious vocabulary

short, clear first paragraph, stating reasons for writing

emotive vocabulary

use of facts to strengthen argument

rule of three emphasises the poor conditions

superlative

consistent development of argument

Exam tip

If you are asked to write an informal letter to a friend or relative, put your address in the top right-hand corner but omit the address of the person you're writing to. Use standard English, but aim for a chatty, friendly tone. End informally, with, for example, 'Love from' or 'See you soon'.

When writing a letter, aim to cover a different aspect of the topic in each paragraph. Finish with a short paragraph that says what you hope will be the result of your letter. For example: 'I hope that local people will be cautious when considering buying a dog and ensure that they have researched its background thoroughly.'

Test yourself

TESTED

Choose *one* of the following tasks to write a letter. Aim to write about 300–400 words.
- Write a letter to the editor of your local paper, expressing your views on whether a proposed music festival should be held in your town.
- Write a letter to your headteacher, giving your views on their recent proposal to lengthen the school day so an extra daily lesson can be added.
- Write a letter to relatives overseas, expressing your desire to stay with them over the next summer holiday.

Answers on p. 103–104

Reports

REVISED

Purpose

The purpose of a report is to inform or advise. They are usually written after a situation has been researched, and the findings are written up in the form of a report. The findings can then be acted on.

Audience

The audience will be the person or group who has commissioned the report. For example, a school council might want a report on energy saving in school. As the report writer is usually writing on behalf of another company or group, avoid the word 'I'. Use phrases such as 'The report has found', 'It is clear that', 'The findings are'. Your tone will be clear, factual and quite formal.

Format

A report is very clearly organised, with a title and separate sub-headings for each section.

The following format is a useful guide:
- Title
- Introduction
- Problems
- Solution
- Conclusion

Exam tip

You will need four or five main aspects that you will look at in your report. For example, for a report on sports facilities in your town, you could look at leisure centres, outdoor sports areas, youth clubs, sports teams and provision for spectators. You would then expand on each with details, facts and examples.

Tasks

Read the following sentences. Decide which are appropriate for a report and which are not. Give reasons for your choices.

1 Dear Sir
2 This report has been prepared in response to the town council's request to assess the use of sporting facilities in Weymouth.
3 I have found a number of problems.
4 People coming to the school will think the place is a tip.
5 It has been found that there are fewer than eight dedicated cycle paths in the whole county.

Answers:

1 'Dear Sir'. ✗ This is the start of a letter, not a report.
2 'This report has been prepared in response to the town council's request to assess the use of sporting facilities in Weymouth.' ✓ Correct, formal tone.
3 'I have found a number of problems.' ✗ Should not use a first person approach. Replace with, 'This report has found …'.
4 'People coming to the school will think the place is a tip.' ✗ Too informal.
5 'It has been found that there are fewer than eight dedicated cycle paths in the whole county.' ✓ Correct, formal tone and clear use of facts.

Test yourself

TESTED ☐

Read the opening sentences of the following report. Continue the report with a paragraph under each of the sub-headings for the **Problems**, **Solutions** and **Conclusion** sections. Aim to write about 300–400 words.

Title: A report on energy saving in Ryder's High School. Report for the headteacher.

Introduction:

This report has been prepared in response to the headteacher's request for an investigation into the current use of energy at Ryder High School. The report will set out the problems involving energy use both inside and outside the school building, make recommendations to resolve these issues and summarise the findings and possible solutions.

Problems:
- Unnecessary lighting:
- Technology:
- Heating:
- After hours:

Solution
- Control lighting:
- Limit use of technology:
- Thermostats:
- After hours:

Conclusion:

Answers on p. 103–104

Typical mistakes

Although writing 'firstly' or 'secondly' is correct, do not continue 'thirdly', 'fourthly', 'fifthly', as this indicates a limited vocabulary. Instead, use phrases such as 'moreover', 'furthermore', 'another point is', 'in addition'.

Speeches

Purpose

A speech gives information, raises an issue, advises or persuades. The exam question will tell you the purpose of the speech and the audience.

Audience

The vocabulary and tone that you decide to use should match the given audience. A speech to your class or a radio phone-in would be more informal than a speech to a group of adults.

Format

You do not need a particular layout for a speech, but will still need to organise your work carefully. You should have clear paragraphs that each deal with a different aspect of your argument.

Planning guide

Be particularly aware of the structure of your speech. In the earlier units on Component 2, Questions 2 and 4, you looked at the way texts are organised in order to maximise their impact. Your speech will need a similar approach.

You could begin your speech by:
- outlining the topic – 'The issue of underage drinking is a serious one'
- having a particular focus or scene – 'On a Saturday night in town …'
- using a quote – 'Our school's liaison officer states that, "Alcohol is hazardous to health."'

Develop the middle section with three or four key points. Support these points with:
- examples – 'It is illegal to buy alcohol under the age of eighteen'
- recognising an opposing view and arguing against it – 'Some people believe … but I consider …'

You could end your speech with:
- a summary of the topic – 'Underage drinking is clearly a problem …'
- a memorable idea – 'Think before you drink'
- advice – 'Don't be influenced by peer pressure'
- a request for action – 'Join our Teen Forum to help spread the message'.

> **rhetoric**: the use of language and techniques designed to have an impressive or memorable effect
>
> **direct address**: appealing directly to the reader through rhetorical questions or use of personal pronouns, such as 'you', 'us' and 'we'; this technique involves the reader
>
> **tripling**: using three examples, such as saying that 'conditions in a zoo are cramped, squalid and unsanitary'; the effect is to strengthen an argument

Task

1 A local radio station has asked for contributions from listeners on the subject of raising the driving age to 18.
   Use the guide you just read to plan ideas for this task.

Task

Think about what sort of tone you would like to use for your speech. You may wish to take quite a serious approach, or, alternatively, a light-hearted, humorous tone. Obviously, this will depend on whether such an approach is suitable for the topic and the audience, but, if you feel that it is, it can be a very effective way to communicate your ideas and interest your audience.

Identify the tone used by the students in the responses below.

They are responding to the following task:

1 An animal rights organisation has called for people to stop keeping animals as pets, claiming that it makes animals dependent on humans and suppresses their natural instincts.

You have decided to give a speech to your year group, expressing your opinions on this.

Student A

> A certain animal rights organisation proposes that no person should ever have a house pet. Their argument is that the relationship between owner and pet is flawed, however kind you are to your pet, because humans are unable to provide the rich, independent lives that animals deserve.

Student B

> For practically my entire life, I've been desperate to have a pet. After finally nagging my beleaguered father into submission, we made the purchase of a dwarf hamster. We named him Dave.
>
> Dave hated us. He hated every second he spent in our non-rodent company. He hated every straw of hay we lovingly provided for him and he hated every last meal we painstakingly prepared for him. His moods, which ranged from brooding contempt to boiling rage, expressed his hatred. It was impossible for him to be less happy in any circumstance than in our arms.

You will have identified that A took a more serious approach than B. Remember that there isn't a 'perfect' tone to take (as long as your choice is suitable to the topic and audience).

Test yourself

TESTED

Your school has raised £1,000 from a recent non-uniform day. The school council is unsure which charity to give the money to. Write a speech, putting the case for your chosen charity. Aim to write about 300–400 words.

Answers on p. 103–104

Leaflets

REVISED

Purpose

If you are asked to write a leaflet, the purpose will be clearly stated for you. A leaflet informs, advises or persuades, such as a safety guide, advice for healthy eating or an advert for a tourist attraction.

Audience

The audience could be adults, teenagers or children. Your language and tone should be suitable for the intended readers. The aim is to keep the tone lively and the content interesting.

Format

A leaflet is clearly organised. It usually includes the following features:
- a heading that states what the leaflet is about
- sub-headings or sections on each aspect of the subject
- bullet points to clarify important ideas.

Do not draw pictures in your leaflet, although you may wish to write in brackets to indicate that the leaflet would have a particular illustration or photograph in.

The use of persuasive or memorable techniques is an important aspect of any leaflet. To be successful, you should be using the techniques that you have practised in this unit. You can also read again the account of Stoke Plaza skate park in the Component 2, Question A2 section of this book (page 59) and use some of the same techniques when you are writing your own leaflet.

> **Exam tip**
>
> Remember to consider the structure of your leaflet. You should engage the reader with examples and give a price for the attraction or ask for a donation in a charity leaflet only at the end of your guide.

Test yourself

TESTED ☐

Read the following extract from a student's Grade 3 response. They were asked to produce a leaflet persuading tourists to visit Ripley Funfair. An examiner wrote, 'The response shows some awareness of purpose, audience and format. The content is relevant and there is some variety of vocabulary, although it is simple. Ideas could be developed as there are few examples and little detail.'

Following the examiner's advice, raise the standard of the answer by completing the table with extra sections that use the persuasive techniques listed. Aim to make the response 300–400 words.

> Ripley Funfair has fun for everyone. There's lots to do in the park. Go on the rides to experience what the fair has to offer (a). People who have gone there say it's great and that more people should go (b). There's a variety of rides and they're all exciting (c). There are restaurants and cafes to have lunch. There's lots of different food on offer (d). Ripley Funfair is easy to get to because it's close to the motorway. It's not too expensive for a day ticket (e).

Ideas	My improvements
a • Emotive language • Direct address	
b • Expert opinion • Quotes	
c • Exclamation • Imperatives	
d • Superlatives • Examples	
e • Facts • Rhetorical question	

Answers on p. 103–104

Reviews

Purpose

A review gives a critical opinion of something, such as a book, film, programme, album, computer game or experience. It does not retell the whole story or reveal the ending, but should interest the reader, then recommend or dissuade. You aim is to inform and entertain.

Audience

The exam question will tell you what audience you are writing for. It is likely to be your own age group who may enjoy similar things to you. You can write in a chatty, friendly style for your peers. Aim to be a little more formal if you are asked to write for an adult audience.

Format

You will need a heading stating what your review is of, then clear paragraphs that follow a plan.

A suggested structure is:
● heading
● introduction giving an overview of the topic being reviewed
● brief plot summary or background to the album, game or experience
● your opinion of main characters, songs on an album or aspects of the game
● comments on any themes
● the best part or feature
● anything you didn't like
● whether you would recommend the subject under review or not.

> **Typical mistakes**
>
> Students often choose to review a subject they think the examiner will like but is something the student does not know much about. Choose a topic you know well so that you can write informatively.

> **Exam tip**
>
> You do not have to be overly serious in the tone of your review. A light-hearted, humorous review can be lively and interesting.

Task

Read the following openings from students' reviews written for a website aimed at teenagers. Annotate the responses with comments on what you think the students do well or aspects that could be improved. You can use the mark scheme for Component 2, Section B in the 'Test yourself' answer section to help you, then read the assessment comments.

Grade 4

> I will be writing a review about Disney films and in particular *Beauty and the Beast*. Disney films have been popular for years and new ones are being made all the time. Disney films were first made in the 1920s but the full-length films started with *Snow White and the Seven Dwarfs*. The film has been re-released many times. Because Disney films are still popular, the stories are still copied. The 2017 film of *Beauty and the Beast* is a perfect example. I wasn't sure Emma Watson would play the role of Belle that well but she really did.

Grade 9

> **Beyoncé's 'Lemonade'**
>
> Inspiring lyrics? Check. Soaring vocals? Check. Explosive tunes? Check. With 'Lemonade', Beyoncé once again reaches for the skies and takes the listener with her. It's her sixth solo album and, arguably, her best.
>
> In 'Lemonade', Beyoncé gives us a unique insight into the trials and experiences that have shaped her inimitable life. From the scathing message of 'Don't Hurt Yourself' to the thoughtful lyrics of 'Hold Up', Beyoncé shows that she'll always be a force to be reckoned with.

Task

1 Choose a favourite film, book or computer game to review. Use the suggested structure and some of the techniques from the Grade 9 response above to write a plan for your chosen review topic.

Test yourself

TESTED ☐

Write the planned review of your favourite film, book or computer game for a teenage magazine. Aim for 300–400 words.

Answers on p. 103–104

How to prepare for the exam

Read online reviews and those in newspapers and magazines. Weekend newspapers often have separate supplements with plenty of reviews included. These will enable you to familiarise yourself with their tone and content so that you can write with confidence in the exam.

Assessment comment

Grade 4 review:

The student is aware of the purpose (review), the audience (teenagers) and the format, although different ideas are all contained in the same paragraph and could be organised more clearly. The content is relevant to a review, with appropriate examples given, although there could be more detail. There is some variety of vocabulary and mostly accurate spelling and punctuation, although there are some errors.

Grade 9 review:

The purpose, audience appeal and format is exactly right for a review. The opening is original and immediately engaging. The content and vocabulary are ambitious and ideas are developed, suggesting that they will be built on still further in the rest of the review. The structure and organisation of ideas are handled well. There are a variety of sentence structures, with confident punctuation and spelling throughout.

Component 3, Spoken language

What this component involves

You will need to give a prepared spoken presentation on a topic and answer questions afterwards.

This is a non-examination unit which is assessed by your teacher. It will be reported as a separate grade (Pass, Merit, Distinction or Not Classified) and will not be part of the result of your English Language GCSE. You will receive one of these grades, not a mark.

Timing

Your presentation should be no longer than ten minutes.

What your teacher is looking for

You will be assessed on:
- your presentation skills
- your ability to listen and respond appropriately to questions following your speech
- your use of Standard English.

In this unit you will revise how to:
- plan and organise your presentation
- deliver your presentation
- respond to questions.

Planning and organisation   REVISED

You are likely to be able to select your own topic, although your teacher may provide ideas or suggestions. Choose a subject that you know well, have an interest in or can research. A debate or discussion may also be offered as an assessment option.

You are not allowed to write out the entire presentation to read from but you can use cue cards and/or a PowerPoint presentation, as long as these just contain prompts.
1 Choose a topic.
2 Jot down what you know about it.
3 Separate these initial ideas into four or five main points.
4 Organise these points into a clear, linked structure.
5 Research to develop these points.

Look back at the advice for speech-writing in Component 2, Section B of this book. This contains ideas for planning and techniques that you can use to maximise the impact of your presentation.

Task

1 You will need to consider structure carefully – that is, the order that you are going to deal with ideas. Read the following ideas for a speech about gender equality. Arrange them in a logical way.

○ Men and women in senior positions.
○ How our own attitudes can make a difference.
○ Men and women's pay in sport.
○ The history of women in the workplace.
○ Maternity and paternity provision.
○ What gender equality is.

A logical order would be:

○ What gender equality is.
○ The history of women in the workplace.
⌐ ○ Men and women's pay in sport.
  ○ Men and women in senior positions.   Note: This order is interchangeable
⌊ ○ Maternity and paternity provision.
○ How our own attitudes can make a difference.

Delivering your presentation

You may have planned an interesting, detailed presentation, but if you do not deliver it in a lively way, you are unlikely to score well.

Tips:
● Speak clearly and audibly.
● Vary your tone so that your feelings and enthusiasm are communicated.
● Maintain a relatively slow pace.
● Speak fluently without using too many fillers, such as 'um' and 'er'.
● Make frequent eye contact with your audience.

Openings

After greeting the audience, you can decide how to start. You could:
● ask a rhetorical question
● explain why you've chosen the topic
● begin with a striking fact or anecdote.

Concluding

Stay confident and focused right up until the end. You could conclude with:
● an overview of the content
● a reference to where the audience can learn more or get involved
● a definitive statement.

Finally, remember to invite questions from the audience.

Responding to questions

Jot down likely questions and practise your answers. If your presentation is informative, you will have pre-empted many questions and can refer your audience to an earlier point or cover it again. (Don't be tempted to snap that you've already explained what they've asked!)

> **Exam tip**
>
> Use some of these sentence starters to help you link your ideas: 'Next ...', 'Consequently', 'Let us also consider ...', 'Some would argue that ...'.

Remember:
- take time to think about a response; buy thinking time with phrases such as 'That's an interesting question' and 'I'm not sure how I feel about that'
- you are not a world expert on your topic; it is perfectly acceptable to say that you do not know an answer to a difficult question.

Mark scheme

Grade	Descriptors
Pass	<ul><li>Straightforward ideas</li><li>Some organisation of content</li><li>Some awareness of audience and purpose</li><li>Simple responses to questions</li></ul>
Merit	<ul><li>Clear and considered ideas</li><li>Well-organised content</li><li>Talk is appropriate and interesting for the audience</li><li>Confident responses to questions</li></ul>
Distinction	<ul><li>Ambitious ideas</li><li>Content is structured for maximum impact</li><li>Task is well suited to the audience and purpose</li><li>Perceptive responses to questions</li></ul>

Test yourself

TESTED

Plan a speech on your leisure activities by using the following steps.
1 Write down four or five main points about your leisure activities.
2 Organise them into a logical structure.
3 Develop each point with details.
4 Write down key sentences and phrases that you would like to use, thinking particularly about how you will start and end.
5 Include some of the techniques you practised in this unit.
6 If possible, link ideas so that your presentation is cohesive.

Answers on p. 103–104

How to prepare for the presentation

To prepare:
- record or film yourself; watch it back to see if it can be improved.
- deliver your presentation to a family member or friend.

Finally, watch a recording of your presentation while referring to the mark scheme. What grade would you award yourself?

Test yourself answers

Using textual references (page 12)

How does the writer convey the impression that teaching is a dangerous job? (5 marks)

This is a 'how' question so there must be explanation of the effect of language or of the writer's techniques.

Award yourself:
- a maximum of 2 marks for shapeless copying
- a maximum of 3 marks for three points from the text
- 4 marks for relevant selection with explanation of effects
- 5 marks for precise selection with analysis of effects.

You could have identified:
- 44.3 per cent of exclusions were due to attacks
- 530 pupils excluded for violent behaviour = shocking statistics suggest a serious problem
- teachers say they feel increasingly unsafe = worsening problem
- students sent home for verbal and racial abuse, misconduct
- and persistent disruptive behaviour = wide range of unruly behaviour.

Component 1, QA1 (page 14)

List five things that you learn about Mr Bellingham.

Award yourself 1 mark each for any five of the following:
- bull-necked
- white-haired
- in his fifties
- he stood on the doorway = vigilant
- speaks 'sharply' = short-tempered
- asks lots of questions = doubtful of what his students tell him
- 'closed his eyes' = he's getting fed up
- gives sharp instructions = controlling
- 'Raising his voice' = strict / becoming increasingly cross
- 'Lesson'll be over' = sarcastic

Component 1, QA2 (page 20)

How does the writer make this extract dramatic? (5 marks)

Mark scheme:

Grade	Descriptors
9	Insightful analysis of the use of drama and of how language and structure are used to achieve varied effects. Purposeful textual references and precise use of subject terminology.
7, 8	Perceptive comments about the dramatic events and analysis of how language and the organisation of events are used to achieve effects, e.g. the passage starts, 'The wind renewed its rage', and develops to show the results of this. Precise textual references and confident use of subject terminology.

Grade	Descriptors
5, 6	Explores the drama in these lines. Analyses how language and the organisation of events are used to achieve effects, e.g. the writer's language highlights the drama unfolding in 'struck', 'thrown', 'carried'. Well-selected textual references and accurate use of subject terminology.
4	Explains how different examples create drama. Begins to look at how language and the organisation of events are used to achieve effects, e.g. 'The boy inside it was screaming' shows fear. Supports with relevant examples. Some use of terminology.
3	Straightforward comments on some of the more obvious examples of drama, e.g. 'the men were pulled across the field'. Straightforward quotations.
1, 2	Expresses a simple, personal opinion of events. Finds simple evidence.

You could comment on the following:
- Adjectives – the 'innocent, comical waggling' of the balloon is a contrast to how dangerous it soon becomes. The 'dangling' lines of the balloon convey a lack of control.
- Verbs – 'struck', 'thrown', 'lifted', 'pulled', 'running', 'screaming', 'struggling', 'shouting' and 'struggling' show how frantic this event was.
- Adverbs – 'suddenly' shows this event was unpredictable and 'frantically' conveys the pilot's desperation.
- Alliteration – 'suddenly stilled' and 'shimmer of strain'. Could argue that this creates a false sense of security in the soft sounds or, alternatively, that the sibilance is rather sinister and ominous.
- Personification – 'The wind renewed its rage.' Sounds like it's a dangerous force with its own mind.

Component 1, QA3 (page 27)

What impressions do you get of Doctor Gordon in this extract?

(10 marks)

You must refer to the text to support your answer.

Mark scheme:

Grade	Descriptors
9	Insightful and subtle analysis of how language and structure are used to achieve a wide range of effects. Purposeful textual references and use of precise subject terminology.
7, 8	Perceptive comments on a range of details about Doctor Gordon. Detailed analysis of how language and structure are used to achieve effects. Precise textual references and confident subject terminology.
5, 6	Makes thoughtful comments about Doctor Gordon, with reference to details. Analyses how language and structure are used to achieve effects. Well-selected evidence and accurate subject terminology.
4	Discusses Doctor Gordon's character, with some attention to how language is used. Relevant quotations and some use of subject terminology.
3	Some explanation of Doctor Gordon's character, with some comments on language choices. Selects straightforward quotations.
1, 2	Simple comments on Doctor Gordon's appearance and character.

You could comment on the following:
- His possible distraction, implied by 'twiddled a silver pencil' and 'tapped his pencil' with the repetition of 'tap, tap, tap.'
- He seems to run a successful practice, with its large leather chair and 'acre of highly polished desk'.

- He is attractive, with 'long and thick' eyelashes. Metaphor used to describe them – 'Black plastic reeds'.
- He is 'so perfect' that he is 'almost pretty'.
- He doesn't inspire trust or confidence in the patient. She dislikes his appearance and attitude.
- He doesn't fit with what the patient wants a psychiatrist to be.
- He waits for the patient to talk.
- He is:
  - young
  - good-looking
  - conceited.

More subtle answers might consider that he may *not* be conceited, but that this is just the patient's view because she doesn't like him.

Component 1, QA4 (page 37)

How does the writer make these lines tense for a reader?   (10 marks)

Mark scheme:

Grades	Descriptors
9	Analyses the subtleties of the techniques used. A wide range of structural techniques are analysed with purposeful evidence to support points.
7, 8	Perceptive analysis of how the writer uses language to create tension. A good range of structural techniques are analysed with precise evidence to support points.
5, 6	Thoughtful analysis of how the writer uses language to create tension. A range of structural techniques are analysed with use of well-selected evidence.
4	Some understanding of how language and organisation create tension. Uses relevant evidence.
3	Awareness of tension. Straightforward textual references.
1, 2	Emerging awareness of the tension in the text, with simple comments made.

Component 1, QA5 (page 42)

Evaluate the way Rob is presented in this passage.   (10 marks)

Mark scheme:

Grades	Descriptors
9	Evaluates the presentation of Rob with subtle insight and detail. Well-selected and purposeful examples explain views. Perceptive analysis of the effect of language and techniques.
7, 8	Evaluates the presentation of Rob clearly and in detail. Chooses precise examples to explain views. Analyses the effect of language and the writer's techniques.
5, 6	Evaluates the presentation of Rob with understanding. Chooses convincing examples to support views. Explains clearly the writer's language choices and techniques.
4	Expresses an opinion of the character of Rob. Supports with relevant references. Some comments on the writer's techniques and language use.
3	Gives a simple opinion of the character of Rob. Supports with straightforward references. May make simple comments on the writer's choice of words.
1, 2	Expresses a simple, personal opinion. Uses basic textual references.

Component 1, Section B Creative prose writing (page 52)

Grade your story on one of the following titles:

a 'Making a Choice'

b 'The Party'

c Write about a time when you let someone down.

d Write a story which begins: 'I looked and saw that the door of the cage was open.'

Your story will be marked out of 40. There are 24 marks available for **content and organisation** and 16 marks for **vocabulary and accuracy**.

Select the band descriptor in each table that best describes the quality of your work.

Communication and organisation:

Grade	Descriptors
9	Plot and characters are developed with flair and originality. Sophisticated structure and original ideas.
7, 8	Creative and original plot and characters. Ambitious structure and ideas.
5, 6	Imaginative plot and characters. Clear structure and thoughtful ideas.
4	General control of plot and characters. Content is organised and interesting.
3	Some control of plot and characters. Some organisation. Attempts to interest the reader.
1, 2	Basic plot and organisation. Simple attempt to interest the reader.

Vocabulary and accuracy:

Grade	Descriptors
9	Varied and interesting sentence structures and totally secure use of grammar. Sophisticated vocabulary is used and spelled correctly. A wide range of punctuation is used with confidence and flair.
7, 8	An effective variety of sentence structures and secure use of grammar. Ambitious vocabulary is used and virtually always spelled correctly. A wide range of punctuation is used confidently.
5, 6	Varied sentence structures and control of grammar. Some ambitious vocabulary choices and mostly secure spelling. A range of punctuation is used accurately.
4	A variety of sentence structures. Vocabulary is developed at times and spelling is usually accurate. Some range of punctuation that is used mostly accurately.
3	Attempts a variety of sentence structures. Some range of vocabulary. Spelling is generally accurate. Some control of punctuation.
1, 2	Simple sentence construction with some inaccuracies. Simple vocabulary. Some spelling and punctuation is accurate.

Component 2, QA1 (page 55)

A1:

a Almost 20 years.

b Northampton.

c They are rising.

Component 2, QA2 (page 62)

How does the writer show that karate is an enjoyable and beneficial sport?

You should comment on:
● what he says
● his use of language and tone
● the structure of the text.   (10 marks)

Mark scheme:

Grades	Descriptors
9	Exacting analysis of the writer's use of language, techniques and tone. Insightful discussion of structure. Purposeful textual references. Precise subject terminology.
7, 8	Perceptive analysis of language, techniques and tone. Discussion of structure. Precise textual references and confident use of subject terminology.
5, 6	Thoughtful analysis of language and techniques. Some attention to tone and/or structure. Well-selected textual references and accurate use of subject terminology.
4	Shows understanding of how language and techniques are used to promote karate. Some relevant quotations to support points. Infrequent subject terminology.
3	Some understanding of how language and techniques are used to promote karate. Straightforward quotations.
1, 2	Some copying of the text with simple comments made.

Component 2, QA3 (page 64)

1 'distress', 'apprehension'

2 'the bedstead'/the bed

Component 2, QA4 (page 69)

What do you think and feel about the prisoner's situation?

You should comment on:
● the conditions in the prison
● how the prisoner's thoughts and feelings are conveyed.   (10 marks)

Mark scheme:

Grade	Descriptors
9	Expresses an insightful opinion, with subtle evaluation of the text and its varied effects, supported by purposeful textual references.
7, 8	Expresses a considered opinion of the prisoner's awful situation, with perceptive evaluation of the text and its effects, supported by precise textual references.
5, 6	Expresses a clear opinion of the prisoner's situation, with thoughtful evaluation of the writer's use of language and techniques, supported by well-selected textual references.
4	Gives an opinion of the prisoner's situation, with some attention to the writer's techniques, supported by relevant quotations.
3	Shows awareness of the prisoner's situation, with straightforward comments on the language used and some quotations to support.
1, 2	Gives a simple personal opinion about the prisoner's situation.

Component 2, QA5 (page 71)

Using information from both texts, what effects can result from saying unkind things about other people? (4 marks)

Both texts are about the effects of being unkind.

Give 1 mark for each of the following:

- Evidence from the first text: 'you may irretrievably injure an innocent person', 'procure for yourself an undesirable name'.
- Evidence from the second text looks only at the effect on the 'troll' themselves: 'they remain dissatisfied', 'ultimately make themselves unhappy'.

Component 2, QA6 (page 77)

Both of these texts are about the methods for calming crying babies.

Compare:
a how the writers feel about these methods
b how they make their views clear to the reader. (10 marks)

Mark scheme:

Grade	Descriptors
9	Makes subtle and sustained comparisons and contrasts. Exacting analysis of the writers' use of language and techniques. Uses purposeful textual references.
7, 8	Careful and perceptive comparisons and contrasts. Close analysis of the writers' use of language and techniques. Uses precise textual references.
5, 6	Detailed comparisons and contrasts. Thoughtful analysis of the writers' use of language and techniques. Uses well-selected textual references.
4	Makes some comparisons between attitudes and ideas. Starts to look at the writers' techniques. Some relevant quotations are used.
3	Shows that the writers' attitudes are different. Some awareness of the writers' language choices and techniques. Straightforward quotations.
1, 2	Identifies basic similarities and/or differences. Finds simple evidence to support.

Ideas that may have been raised are as follows:

Text A
- The method is unexpected.
- It is unusual.
- It needs to be seen to be believed.
- It has surprisingly quick results.

The writer seems to admire/be impressed by these methods.

Text B
- Loud and violent methods are inappropriate.
- They cause pain and upset and should be avoided.
- The writer has witnessed these methods.
- They are too extreme.

The writer disapproves of these methods.

Component 2, Section B Transactional and persuasive writing (pages 82, 85, 87, 88, 90, 91, 93, 96)

The tasks will be marked out of 20. There are 10 marks available for **content and organisation** and 10 marks for **accuracy**.

Use the following mark scheme to assess your work on the 'Test yourself' tasks set on the article (pages 82, 85), formal letter (page 87), report (page 88), speech (pages 90, 96), leaflet (page 91) and review (page 93).

Select the band descriptor in each table that best describes the quality of your work.

Communication and organisation:

Grade	Descriptors
9	Purpose, audience and format is perfectly matched to task. Original content. A wide range of ideas are developed with flair and originality. Sophisticated structure and organisation of ideas.
7, 8	Purpose, audience and format is precisely matched to task. Ambitious content. A range of ideas are developed with details and are original and creative. Ambitious structure and organisation of ideas.
5, 6	Purpose, audience and format is secure. Thoughtful content. A range of ideas with appropriate examples to support. Clear structure and connected ideas.
4	Clear awareness of purpose, audience and format. Relevant content. Some development of ideas and appropriate examples. Uses paragraphs to organise work and connects ideas.
3	Awareness of purpose, audience and format. Mostly relevant content. Starting to develop ideas, with some examples used. Evidence of organisational techniques.
1, 2	Basic awareness of purpose, audience and format. Some relevant content. Simple communication of mostly personal ideas. Basic organisation with few or no paragraphs.

Vocabulary and accuracy:

Grade	Descriptors
9	Varied and interesting sentence structures and totally secure use of grammar.
	Sophisticated vocabulary is used and spelled correctly.
	A wide range of punctuation is used with confidence and flair.
7, 8	An effective variety of sentence structures and secure use of grammar.
	Ambitious vocabulary is used and virtually always spelled correctly.
	A wide range of punctuation is used confidently.
5, 6	Varied sentence structures and control of grammar.
	Some ambitious vocabulary choices and mostly secure spelling.
	A range of punctuation is used accurately.
4	A variety of sentence structures.
	Vocabulary is developed at times and spelling is usually accurate.
	Some range of punctuation that is used mostly accurately.
3	Attempts a variety of sentence structures.
	Some range of vocabulary. Spelling is generally accurate.
	Some control of punctuation.
1, 2	Simple sentence construction with some inaccuracies.
	Simple vocabulary. Some spelling and punctuation is accurate.